Building A Championship Culture

Using lessons from the game I love to WIN in business and in life!

By: Dave Strand *with Reji Laberje*

In The News

"What a great program! Everybody really liked what Dave had to say!"

~Waukesha County Business Alliance (WCBA)

Access the Electronic Resource Hub

Scan the QR code to see a clip of Dave speaking at the WCBA!

"It's about what you can do with GREAT people!"

~Bob & Brian Radio Show, 102.9 FM, The HOG, Milwaukee, WI

This work is based on the experiences of an individual. Every effort has been made to ensure the accuracy of the content.

Quantity order requests can be emailed to:
publishing@rejilaberje.com
Or mailed to:
Reji Laberje Author Programs
Publishing Orders
234 W. Broadway Street
Waukesha, WI 53186

Strand, David
Building A Championship Culture
Contributor: Reji Laberje, Reji Laberje Author Programs, LLC.
Interior Design: Michael Nicloy
Cover design: Carl Flath, Andrea Strand
"About The Authors" photos courtesy of Kimberly Laberge. All other photos courtesy of David Strand unless otherwise noted.
ISBN: 151741475X
ISBN-13:978-1517414757
BISAC Codes:
  Business & Economics/General – BUS000000
  Business & Economics/Management – BUS041000
  Business & Economics/Leadership - BUS071000

Author Programs, LLC.

www.rejilaberje.com

Dedication

I dedicate this book to my family! To my parents Jerry Strand, and Ann Peters. To my brother Kurt Strand, and sister Sheri Polczynski. To my children Ryan Strand, Troy Strand, and Catelynn Strand. To My Wife Andrea who is my soulmate!

My life is consumed by business, meetings and hundreds of employees and associates that require my time and it often leaves our family short of quantity time. Thank you to all of you for ensuring that the times we do have, are quality.

Table Of Contents

Foreword

"Building A Championship Culture" was born naturally out of the professional journey Dave Strand experienced in his time with Wisconsin Oven Corporation. In June of 2014, co-author Reji Laberje had the opportunity to hear him speak and share the lessons necessary to helping great people accomplish even greater things. Immediately, she knew there was a message here that needed to be heard, not just by industrial leaders, but all professional leaders and—in reality—all adults.

Championship culture is, at its core, about championing the people of great visions to show them that they are capable of achieving those visions! Dave Strand manages to be that champion in his company and his life and he manages to document the lessons of that objective here in this book for others to be able to apply.

"Building A Championship Culture" is a Reji Laberje Author Programs interactive text. Throughout the book, you will find QR codes that will provide a little more insight into what is being shared. Find a free QR scanner for your smart device via a search through your device's app store. Then, you can scan the QR code with your smart device to discover the online resource. In addition, all of the information from the QR codes can be found on the Electronic Resource Hub for *"Building A Championship Culture."* Want to try it out? Visit the Resource Hub through the below QR code:

"Building A Championship Culture" Electronic Resource Hub
Good luck building YOUR championship culture!

Building A
Championship Culture

FIRST HALF

On January 3, 1993, Rich Stadium in Buffalo, New York was a depressing place to be for those who called Buffalo home.

It was a playoff day for the Buffalo Bills, but the stadium had such low attendance that the game, played against the Houston Oilers, wasn't even being broadcast by the local affiliates.

Radio stations were likely quickly tuned out as the Oilers dominated the game early on. Warren Moon, who was—at the time—a five-time pro-bowl quarterback, was on his game with 220 yards passing to help his team reach many first half touchdowns. One of his drives took nine minutes off the clock and—in all—he kept his offense on the field for more than twenty-one of the first thirty minutes of play.

The opening drive of the game ended with a three-yard pass to wide receiver Haywood Jeffires who brought the initial score to a 7–0 lead over Buffalo. Jeffires' touchdown was answered by the Oilers' Steve Christie. His thirty-six yard field goal put Houston on the board with 3 points.

BUT—Moon took control again in a drive that had Webster Slaughter scoring a touchdown. There was nothing from the Bills. Then, Curtis Duncan scored ANOTHER 7 points for Houston! With only 1:15 left in the half, the Oilers drove for another touchdown! Fellow pro-bowl teammate Jeffires was at it again with a twenty-seven yard reception.

The Oilers strolled into the locker room with their 28–3 halftime lead over Buffalo in Buffalo.

The game wasn't over . . .

A Championship Vision

A Player Is Drafted

"The measure of who we are is what we do with what we have."

~NFL Great Vince Lombardi

"*MONEY GAME!* It's on!"

That's how a lot of summers started when I was growing up. My dad, Jerry, had been working at a factory where he had gotten a hold of these glossy laminated pieces of paper that he brought home. I had never seen papers like that. I loved the feel of them and thought it was cool how you could write on it; so, I made "money." There were different denominations--$1.00, $5.00, $10.00—and every bill had my signature on it, *Dave Strand*, so it couldn't be counterfeited.

I lived in a perfect neighborhood for hanging out and growing up because we were all around the same age and we got along. When summer kicked off, a group of us would start our annual money game. My brother, Kurt, still talks about it today. Each of the neighbor kids and my brother and I would get the same amount of money in the beginning of the summer. Then, we ran our own little "businesses."

We had a restaurant, a casino, a gas station, and one kid—who had spent a lot of time with his own dad in the bar—decided his business would be the local tavern. He served Kool-Aid and water and, sometimes, other friends would pretend they were drunk. They copied the people they had seen in this era where men still took their boys with them into the bars to hang out while they had their drinks. In the money game casino, they threw dice around and pretended to gamble.

Our gas station was pretty cool. We used emptied Tic-Tac containers filled with water. We would open the little pop-top and tape it upside down on our bike handlebars so that the water would slowly run out. The only place to refill our Tic-Tac water fuel was at the *Money Game* gas station.

Every once in a while, a couple of guys would rob one of the businesses and that's where I came in; I was the sheriff. As the oldest in the neighborhood, I was the law. I would light up my handlebar lights and call into my little megaphone. It was all part of the game. The "culprits" would ride off into the woods and I'd chase them down on my bike, retrieve the stolen money, and throw the criminals-of-the-day into money game jail. The next day, after a jail breakout, those kids would maybe run their own legitimate businesses if they felt like being businessmen instead of robbers that day.

ALL. SUMMER. LONG.

"*MONEY GAME!* It's on!"

It was a little economy all its own, imitating what we saw, running the world how we assumed it must be run. I was about ten-years old at the time. I think that was my first business model.

I was always watching the world through my *Money Game*-sized window into the economy.

The wealth that lay within seldom stayed within. There were always cycles when people didn't necessarily invest their money correctly. They took a lot of risk and they lost all of their money. The *Money Game*, like any economy, fluctuated from time-to-time and was full of bad decisions. There were a few of those who made some really great decisions, too and it was kind of neat to see how different people reacted in different ways to their wealth or lack of wealth.

There were guys who worked hard at gas stations and restaurants. There were workers who served and worked in our little community. There was also everything from bank robberies and jailbreaks to drunkenness (in its sugar-high, Kool-Aid form, that was) and casino losses.

I policed our *Money Game* and, from that position, I learned that it was just as important to make the right plays with money as it was to make right plays in my neighborhood sport leagues.

Those sport leagues began as a result of being my father's son. As I begin to share my championship vision, my dad has just turned seventy-one. Dad had been an All-Time Quarterback when he was younger and I don't remember a time when he didn't throw the ball around with Kurt and I as kids. My brother and I would play against one another and Dad was QB for both of us. I was a little bigger and a year and a half older, so I'd usually win, but sometimes Dad would pull out a trick play, just to keep me on my toes.

I'll never forget the *Flea-Flicker* Dad did with Kurt. Dad passed the ball to my brother so I—of course—ran all out at him; then Kurt passed back to my dad! What was I supposed to do? I sure as heck had never tackled my dad!

Yeah. Dad definitely tried (and usually succeeded) to even the odds between us from time-to-time.

top: lining up against Kurt
bottom: Dad throwing the long pass

> **"Competitor"**
>
> *Somebody that you need to find a way to beat with intellect, physicality, strategy, and assistance from your team.*
>
> *~Dave's Definitions*

Not all of the neighbors had dads who hung out with them and, with Dad's great arm, our home became the place to be for all of the kids after school. Dad must have thrown thousands of passes in the "warmer" Wisconsin months. We played baseball, too, and ended up becoming sort of a neighborhood league headquarters for all of our sports. I organized all the guys into teams of four players, each . . . real teams! We created a league schedule, kept football stats, tracked yards as best we could, and noted leading passers and rushers.

Growing up as a child for me was a mixed bag of up and downs. I cherish the memories of my dad always taking time after a Packer game to play some one-on-one with my brother and I. Dad always worked and three of us had Mom's love and passion for our family; she was always home taking care of us. Mom was resourceful and often came up with creative ways to earn extra money for the family. She did crafts and picked up jobs when things got tight. Mom was the one who got us to church and made sure that we had a Christian upbringing. Dad slept in on Sundays to recharge his battery for another week of work. This was just life and it seemed normal to me.

Dad was the disciplinarian and mom was always there preparing the nest. As a family, we enjoyed dinner together and prayed together before meals and bed. As children, we always kissed our parents good night and would exchange the words, "I love you."

Both of my parents came from tough upbringings with stern parents who weren't as open with their affections or words of love. Maybe that's why my dad's way of showing his true love came through in his playing of sports with us.

In the tiny village area between the farming towns of East Troy, Wisconsin and Mukwonago, Wisconsin, we were the living picture of American childhood every day until that afternoon in seventh grade when it all changed.

My brother and I came home from school.

There was a roast in the oven.

Dad was sitting at the kitchen table.

He had a letter in his hand.

It was a *"Dear John"* letter.

Mom was leaving.

She was taking our sister with her.

Everything would be different.

That stupid roast in the oven . . . I don't know why I remember that, but life changing moments tend to stick with you in great detail. The first time a son sees his dad crying—wrecked—that's a moment that freezes in time. We had no clue. My brother and I didn't know there was anything wrong. We didn't understand what was going on. We were just heartbroken, my dad was really going through a tough time and—little did we know—so was my mom.

Even though the marriage failed, as parents, Mom and Dad—in their own way—played like champions for our family. It's a true miracle that they fought and struggled through their own challenges and were able to raise three children that have all been very successful. My brother has an incredibly hard working spirit that finds a way to win day after day. My sister Sheri is the first Strand that has ever achieved a master's degree and we're so proud of her. Today, all of us are close. My mother's and father's ways of showing their love instilled an incredible value for affection and compassion in all three of us.

On the day of that letter, though, Dad was at the start of a long-fought comeback. We had a tough road ahead of us and it was hard; I think it was hardest on Dad. It got pretty ugly going through the divorce. We saw things kids shouldn't have to see their parents go through. Emotions run hot and there's this pendulum that swings back and forth between anger and not giving a crap.

Plus, the process cost a lot of time . . . and money. We had never been rich, but now things were really tight and Dad was around even less because he had to work more in order to pay for it all. The judge gave us a choice about who to live with when we got to that part of the whole family-breaking process, but he also told us that there was no way the state (at that time) would take a two-year-old away from her mother. I had looked after Sheri. How could somebody take her from us?

Divorce is normal in today's society - even when I was a kid; so, people tend to think it doesn't need explaining. But it still hurt and didn't make sense to us. My brother and I, in youthful misunderstanding and naiveté, were pretty bitter about Mom's choice, so we stayed with Dad. I loved my little sister and it wouldn't be until adulthood that I really had the opportunity to redevelop a close relationship with Sheri.

Things were tough for Kurt and me from the divorce all the way through graduation. I don't want to speak for my brother, but I know I didn't care much about school, anymore. Dad was working a lot of hours in this new era, so there wasn't really accountability for grades or attendance. The only things that kept me active in school at all were sports. I even kept that neighborhood league going.

top: with Mom and Kurt
bottom: (left) with Dad; (right) with my sister, Sheri

Profile of a Teammate: Kurt Strand

Joe Namath famously said, *"Football is a team game. So is life."* I don't think I could have gotten through my own early life without a great teammate like the one I had in my younger brother, Kurt.

As a kid, Kurt wanted to be with me all the time. The thing is, I didn't mind when we were playing sports. I tried not to be that "big brother" who was too cool for younger siblings. (Of course, that went through cycles, too!) When our parents split, Kurt and I had a desire to stay together even more than we did to stay with one parent or another. I think, if I had chosen to go with mom, he would have joined me. We had an unbreakable bond of brotherhood. Not that we didn't try to break *each other* from time to time. Did we fight? Hell yes! I remember chasing him around the front yard in an early morning fight that darn near resulted in us missing the bus before school.

Deep down, I think I had an ulterior motive in spending so much time with my younger brother: *Kurt made me better.*

Today, my brother works with the Pennsylvania-based company, Pace Industries in the Airo Division doing die casting for Harley Davidson parts. He's the expert in **polishing**, **brushing**, and **chroming** out America's bikes to make them into head-turning masterpieces. He also teaches others the techniques needed to make these parts shine. He's actually had a lifetime of experience in this sort of work.

Dad sometimes says that he shouldn't have been teaching us such a competitive nature, that it drew us apart. In reality, at least in the long run, it drew us *to* success, rather than *from* one another.

When Dad made Kurt face a bigger and older brother on the field, Kurt had to learn how to play smarter and in adversity. When Dad helped my brother develop creative plays, I was taught that every win had to be earned. I couldn't expect it because of age or size. Nothing is promised.

Brush. Brush. Kurt helped to refine my game and my mind for life outside of the game.

As kids, we used to play a lot of video games together. We were really tight. Those times sitting with our Atari controllers were different than the times spent playing sports together. It was quiet . . . just the two of us. Those were special bonding days. They were still very competitive, though. I once held the high score for what seemed like eternity on Space Invaders. One day, I watched nervously as Kurt approached my high score . . . he was ALMOST THERE! Quick thinking kicked in! I ran down the stairs to the power box and killed the main power breaker to the entire house. Poor Kurt; had his visions of a sweet defeat of his big brother disappear from in front of his very eyes. That resulted in a heck of a fist fight and Kurt landed a few haymakers, to say the least. So, maybe except for Space Invaders, we enjoyed the small moments.

Polish. Polish. Kurt helped to refine my game and my mind for life outside of the game.

When Kurt was in his junior year of high school, and I was in my senior year, we had an opportunity to play a few games together, on the same team. We worked together, rather than against one another, and we shared the end goal of winning **as a team**.

Like chrome-plating, Kurt made me stronger. He helped to refine my game and my mind for life outside of the game.

I feel lucky in many ways in life, and being older than Kurt, I could have been a step ahead, but—without him—I might not have been able to move ahead. Kurt was so often the teammate I could count on to give me a leg up to take that step up. That's a true teammate. Teammates make one another smoother, better, stronger. Brush. Polish. Plate.

Today, the success Kurt and I each have is due, in no small part, to one another. Kurt and I are now much closer as brothers. We have a special bond that you'll never break. I think that we'll both always be managers of people, rather than processes, as a result of our competitive upbringing, always seeking to bring out the best in our teams. Always seeking to brush, polish, plate, and create masterpieces.

In more parallel words from Joe Namath, *"Pressure just makes you go a little more. I kind of like pressure."*

top: (left) Kurt and I running plays in the living room
(right) playing football in the Wisconsin winter
bottom: reunited with Kurt on a trip to Pennsylvania, 2015

****

By the time I was a freshman in high school, finances had gotten pretty tough for us. My brother and I had no money and Dad didn't have any to give us. We wanted our own uniforms, jerseys, and equipment like other teams had, but that stuff didn't come cheap, even then.

One afternoon, in Earth Science Class, I bought a 50¢ candy bar from a classmate. I bit into the caramel-filled chocolate and peeled the label back. It said, *"If you want to earn money for your organization . . . "*

The answer to all of our problems! I filled out the wrapper with my dad's information and our Miramar-Mukwonago League as the organization.

I was about to start my *next* big business venture!

Back at that time, there were no credit checks and the government wasn't busy shutting down children's lemonade stands. A pen and a candy wrapper were all it took to kick off our fundraiser. And, by kick it off, I mean that boxes and boxes of chocolate arrived on my front door step. The UPS guy had to wonder what was going on when a teenager signed for cases of M&Ms, Heath Bars, Caramel Bars, and Crunch Bars.

My bedroom smelled like a confectionary, so my little business wasn't a secret I could keep for long. I had to come

Lessons From The League Of Leaders!

"If you're not a risk-taker, you should get the hell out of business."

~Ray Kroc, McDonald's Founder

clean to my dad and let him know what was going on. Since the legally-binding, caramel-coated, candy wrapper was in his name, anyway, he became our backer. The incoming cash from candy bar sales would go to Dad and his checks would go back to the candy distributors.

I had all of the guys from our league over and I would distribute the goods to them, keeping track of who had what inventory. This whole idea of having actual money to spend was new to a lot of us. We weren't rich kids; we had all been used to just getting by. But, candy bar sales had us living like what we thought were fat cats.

We ordered *more* inventory!

Selling became an addiction. We bought jerseys. We were able to afford all of our equipment. And, honestly, we were a bunch of young men who maybe did a few things with the money that we shouldn't have done. My brother gambled over cards at lunch. And maybe not every article of clothing I got qualified as a uniform.

Eventually, our little taste of power proved more than we could handle. We were in the red. Some guys weren't turning in their money at all. I had to bust people in the hallways. *'Richard! Where's the money? You only gave me like a third of the stock you took!'*

The bills were coming. The payables were coming! WE.WERE.IN.TROUBLE.

Like any big brother in trouble, I knew it was time to bring out the big guns, or, in this case, the younger, cuter guns of my kid brother, Kurt. Now, the M&Ms, Caramel Bars, and Crunch Bars went 50¢ apiece. We were always left with the Heath bars, though, and those fundraising candy bars went for only 25¢ apiece. The guys and I sent Kurt, adorable as he could be, door-to-door, with all of the leftover Heath bars.

"Would you like to buy some candy bars for the Miramar-Mukwonago baseball *(or sometimes football)* league?" He'd ask. "We're trying to get some uniforms."

Who was going to say "no" to him?

"That will be 50¢."

One flash of Kurt's *"Leave It to Beaver"* grin and we were doubling our way out of debt.

This became a regular routine. Kurt bailed us out so many times and we just kept reordering and reordering and reordering. We were the candy bar hookup for two solid years!

Entrepreneurialism all started right there in the fundraiser:

- Understanding receivables
- Understanding payables
- Understanding how to get out of a difficult situation
- Realizing the importance of following business ethics *(If you didn't, you'd get caught at a loss!)*

My inner-entrepreneur was in the game.

DID YOU KNOW?

IN 1934, THE FOOTBALL GOT IT'S ELONGATED, THINNER SHAPE TO ENCOURAGE A GOOD GRIP AND AERODYNAMICS FOR THE PASSING GAME.

ASK YOURSELF IF YOU NEED TO MAKE ANY CHANGES TO MEET YOUR ULTIMATE GOALS!

Joining The Team

> *"How one handles success or failure is determined by their early childhood."*
>
> **~Comedic Actor Harold Ramis**

If the *Money Game* taught me about the economy and the Miramar-Mukwonago League fundraiser taught me entrepreneurialism, it was running the league games that taught me how to run a company. I got to know the guys in the neighborhood well. As kids, we were playmates; then, we became teammates. I really became familiar with the guys through our little football league.

left: in our league, I was QB...and the Commish

Robert Grant. What a kid! He was not the oldest kid. He was not the fastest kid. Robert Grant just was this stocky young guy who loved football. That would be the end of the story with no lesson to be learned except that Robert Grant was the leading rusher in our league every game, every season, every year. Robert Grant played with heart. This kid did not have a lot of natural athletic ability but just enough of it to get by.

He avoided every tackle.

He would spin.

He would stiff-arm.

He would do whatever it took to get wherever he had to get.

What made this pretty special is that Robert Grant had a pretty tough life at home. He didn't get a lot of accolades or affections, but when we played that game, he was the hero and we would really pump him up. My brother and I would celebrate his victories and he felt really good about that. Sometimes, we would call him Robert "Walter Payton" Grant and it was one of the greatest parts of the game to be able to cheer him on. He turned out okay in life and I'd like to think that he got a taste for victory from some of those early games.

> **Lessons From The League Of Leaders!**
>
> *I think the thing about that was I was always willing to work; I was not the fastest or biggest player but I was determined to be the best football player I could be on the football field and I think I was able to accomplish that through hard work."*
>
> *~Jerry Rice, Former NFL Running Back*

Then, there was Chad Kawczynski and that kid was fast! He was younger than all of us, but he could pull off a flea-flicker play that would always burn everybody. Chad had hands. He could run like lightning. It was kind of neat to have this Kawczynski kid who was the youngest in the neighborhood performing so well.

As the oldest in the group, it kind fell on me to teach the guys how the cheer on others and how to celebrate. I always wanted to bring out their bests and I got just as much satisfaction out of leading them as I did out of being the one to make the plays.

> *"Effort"*
>
> *Giving life everything you've got. Everything inside of you keeps going until you cross the finish line. Life is a competition. It's an all-out, full-blown obstacle course.*
>
> *~Dave's Definitions*

I certainly didn't know it, then, but all of those times messing around in the neighborhood were times spent preparing for leadership and for life. I can look back as an adult and see lessons from childhood that still show in my style, today.

My early life was like the first quarter and the lessons I learned were a touchdown I could carry forward toward victory.

1st Quarter TOUCHDOWN

1. *Be prepared for fluctuating economies.*

2. ***Everybody*** *has obstacles to overcome; overcoming them is a choice.*

3. *Teammates are meant to sharpen one another.*

4. *If you don't work smart from the start, you'll have to work harder in the end.*

5. *Never underestimate a strong will to win.*

6. *Don't presume (a lack of) abilities based on age, alone.*

7. <u>*Be a friend:*</u> *Celebrating **others'** victories can feel like a personal victory.*

~Leadership Lessons From Outside The Leadership Role

DID YOU KNOW?

THE HOME TEAM IN AN NFL GAME MUST PROVIDE 36 BALLS FOR PLAY.

BE CERTAIN YOUR TEAMS HAVE WHAT THEY NEED TO EARN A WIN!

A Cinderella Story

Making First String

"When you're good at something, you'll tell everyone. When you're great at something, they'll tell you."
~NFL Record-Setting Running Back Walter Payton

Wisconsin Oven Corporation was founded in 1973 and, little did I know, thirteen years later, I would have my first day of work there. I was only seven-years old and—if you'd asked me—I would have assumed they made the kind of stoves and ovens that you could find in the kitchen of any typical home. In reality, Wisconsin Oven was making ovens for the industrial world.

Access the Electronic Resource Hub:

Scan the QR code to see more about industrial ovens

These industrial heat-treating ovens were used to temper and stress relieve steel and aluminum, cure powder coating, and provide heat-treating. Just about anything you touch today requires some heat, from laminate signage to a pair of slacks that require de-wrinkling in clothing factories. Wisconsin Oven sells ovens to everybody from printing companies to Ford and Boeing. Industrial heat is needed in more places than most people realize.

In 1973, Wisconsin Oven was just a little upstart company in East Troy, Wisconsin with about a dozen employees. It didn't change much from that status over the next ten years.

I, however, did change. When I was seventeen, and full of teenage angst, my Dad and I had an argument and I left home to go live with my cousin for a bit. I went from selling candy for a living to discovering that you couldn't live on fundraisers, even when sold at 50¢ a bar.

My first job was at Alpine Valley in East Troy. Alpine Valley was a skiing lodge that served as a concert venue in the few Wisconsin months without snow. I started as a dishwasher, but I eventually got an opportunity to work as a table busser, too. Before long my friends were all giving me their shifts. I would work day shift as a dishwasher and night shift bussing tables. It turned out that all of my friends were giving me their hours because they'd only gotten a job at Alpine Valley so that they could ski for free in the winter, and see free concerts in the summer. After that career, my cousin worked at a company that made dumpsters and he got me in as a pre-paint dumpster washer there.

I would get off of school on a work pass at 1:30 in the afternoon, work until 2:00 or 3:00 in the morning and head back to school at 6:00 in the morning. At school, I took basic math, choir, gym, and anything else I could to minimally get by. Then, I'd head back to work. I started making some good money and learned some basic skills.

At just twenty-years old, I got married, made amends with Dad, and needed to find a "grown up" place to work.

On a crazy stormy day in 1986, there was this Wisconsin Oven Corporation in East Troy's Industrial Park that I'd heard was accepting applications. I didn't know much about them, but I ran to the front door of the building in the midst of the downpour and asked for an application. I was cold and soaking wet when I filled out the paperwork, then I left and went back to my other job.

I didn't hear anything back.

Another day and I still didn't hear anything.

Then, I called them . . . every day.

"*Did you get my application?*"

"*Are you doing any interviews?*"

I called Every. Single. Day. For twenty days.

"*Just checking to see if you got my messages.*"

"*What did you think of my application?*"

Lessons From The League Of Leaders!

Nothing in this world can take the place of persistence. Talent will not: nothing is more common than unsuccessful men with talent. Genius will not; unrewarded genius is almost a proverb. Education will not: the world is full of educated derelicts. Persistence and determination alone are omnipotent.

~U.S. President Calvin Coolidge

Finally, and probably because I was a pain in the butt more than the impressiveness of my soggy resume, they opted to call me in for an interview. After all, it was easier than the probably equally deserved restraining order!

On my first interview with Wisconsin Oven, I sat down with a man named Bruce Champion. He asked about my skill set and, where specific tasks were concerned, I didn't really have a lot of experience to bring to the table, but my three weeks of calls after a drenched application day had preceded me as reputation.

Bruce said to me, "80% of your success is coming in every day and giving 110%. The other 20% would come from them."

The way I saw it, that gave me 210% to work with, which had to be better than the money I was making as a dumpster washer. It was a $2.00 cut in pay from the dumpster factory that was a dead end shop full of guys doing drugs on the job. I took the job for $5.50 per hour! I also took all the overtime I could find. I had started a family already and I'd learned from my own upbringing that hard work was necessary to fatherhood.

Access the Electronic Resource Hub

Scan the QR code to see more about Wisconsin Oven

I also took every unclaimed, unappreciated task they'd offer.

In the beginning of my tenure with Wisconsin Oven, my days started early. I'd wake around 3:00 in the morning and take care of the morning feeding of my infant son, Ryan, so that I could give some home help before getting to the factory. Bruce had created an early morning job for me of entering the inventory of our signed out parts in Lotus Notes. At the time, these were called our "white sheets." (My, how times have changed!) The data entry included what the part number was, a description of the part, and who signed the part out. It was a different era and, before that daily task, I had never even turned on a computer in my life, or seen a very-advanced-at-the-time floppy disc. Bruce literally had to draw out every key stroke for me and it took awhile to even be able to locate those keys on the computer. I spent three hours on the data entry work before moving from white sheets to the dirtiest work in the factory.

Shearing steel, washing ovens, and insulating the ovens were and still are the three dirtiest jobs in the factory. I did them all: steel shearing, washing ovens, and insulating ovens. These tasks made up my day job from 7:00 in the morning until 4:30 in the afternoon.

I learned that there is a process to everything a factory does and, no matter how minor the process seems to be, it's critical to the overall success of the project. These were the crap duties, but they were necessary for the end product. Each one of us is a significant part of the body of a finished product. There are no minor parts; we all equal that body.

Then, at the end of the day, I could paint. Because, you know, there might have been a speck of me left that wasn't yet filthy.

Painting meant fumes, so we couldn't do it until after hours unless we wanted the workers passing out all over the factory floor. I would paint until 9:00 at night.

There are a lot of pictures of me with my kids when they're babies. I'm asleep in most of them, with blackened hands, reddened skin, and flecks of color for good measure.

I learned about working longer and harder in those early days at Wisconsin Oven, but Bruce wanted to help me to work smarter, too. Unless I began to gain some of the skill set necessary to the larger operations and larger body parts of the company I had joined, I'd spent my life working eighteen-hour days.

I needed to learn how to *build* those big ovens.

I needed to learn how to weld.

There's a reason technical and vocational skills are called gold-collared jobs. We're still a country that needs to build things and builders are harder than ever to find.

Bruce sent me to tech school at night, after working each day. I kept up that schedule for a full year. I still did the white sheets in the mornings. I'd work until 4:00 in the afternoon doing the dirty jobs. I'd get to school at 5:00 in the evening and take classes until 9:00 or 10:00 three nights out of the week.

I didn't have a lot of self-confidence, but I worked hard at Wisconsin Oven and at school. I was younger than a lot of the guys in the plant and, as a result, always felt a little bit shy. I just wanted my work ethic speak for itself. I had one welding instructor, though, who told me I was the best he'd seen and I needed to ask for a raise. That built confidence within me, but I still didn't tell them I needed the raise. I did let the leaders see my work, though, and I let the work do the talking.

For a little while during this phase of building ovens, I was incredibly happy as a *company man* . . . a technician, really. I became the highest producer of ovens and continued working long hours. I was getting regular raises. I remember the first $3.00 per hour raise I got. I drove home at probably ninety miles per hour to tell my family about it at lunch.

Just because I was doing well, though, didn't mean the company was. The economy was slowing down. There wasn't enough work to fill the day and I was afraid that I'd be laid off. The supervisor of the factory floor at the time assured me that I was going to be fine. Some guys slowed down to stretch out the work, but it wasn't my style. I wasn't going to slow down just because the work did. That didn't play out well for me, at first.

One morning . . .

Before the end of the week, I was sent home. There was no work left to be done.

I quit.

I grabbed my toolbox.

I got in my car.

Over lunch . . .

I drove over to our closest competitor and got an immediate interview.

When I toured the shop floor, a former worker from Wisconsin Ovens saw me and pulled over the interviewer.

In a moment, he returned to me and said, "Tom says I must hire you because you're the hardest working guy he's ever known."

It so happened that I had just finished doing some off-site work at Wisconsin Oven, which was paid at $1.00 per higher than usual, so the check stub in my pocket read $15.50 per hour, rather than my typical $14.50 per hour pay. I was immediately offered a pay increase to $16.00 per hour.

That afternoon . . .

I still had to give my official notice, so I returned to Wisconsin Oven and went into Bruce Champion's office. I told him I couldn't stay in a company that promised I wouldn't be laid off and, later in that same week, laid me off. I explained how I was already offered a pay increase by our competitor.

Bruce wouldn't hear of it. He called the owner, Hank, who was in Europe and the two had a short conversation followed by Bruce's offer:

"How about I make you the working plant manager at $18 per hour and you can still get overtime?"

That night . . .

I went home and told my family about the raise and promotion. I was a leader now, for the first time since my Miramar-Mukwonago Football League days.

The next day . . .

I would begin my journey toward **building a championship culture**.

My early career moves were like the second quarter and the lessons I learned were a touchdown I could carry forward toward victory.

2nd Quarter TOUCHDOWN

1. Give 110% effort. Everybody can give 100%. Show that you can go BEYOND the expectation.
2. Build trust with your leadership so that they invest in you.
3. Work smarter AND harder; BOTH are productive.
4. Lead by example; somebody may be noticing you.
5. Work with a sense of urgency for what you are accomplishing.
6. Don't let anything go to your head; let your work speak for itself.
7. <u>Be a friend:</u> Be kind to those above you; you may be surprised at their kindness expressed in return.

~Leadership Lessons As One Of The Team

****

I was a bit of an experiment for Wisconsin Oven Corporation. Having somebody who both manages and works as part of the team—a working supervisor—was a brand new role. I discovered what kind of leader I would one day become. Being plant manager was probably one of the times I had the most fun in my entire career. I was still working with my hands, so it was like I was a player coach on the field and calling the plays. I only led others to do the work that I was willing to do, myself.

In those early leadership days, we found ourselves in a situation where we had a very upset customer because the equipment was not working right in the field. We had spent a lot of overtime in the shop and nobody wanted to go out in the field; people were burnt out. I had what I thought was a motivational, kick-in-the-butt speech to get us moving.

"We gotta stop effing complaining and just get it done!" I said in my best Al Pacino impression.

It felt more like a threat to them. At the time, I was shop supervisor and I was in the trenches with them putting in a ton of hours. I wouldn't have asked them to do what I couldn't, but one of the guys I knew for a long time told me that pulling out the "f-bomb" was demoralizing. Ouch. Some of the guys even thought I'd turn into a tyrant and they'd consider working somewhere else.

I'd never had any training, so I had to learn this lesson. I changed my management style in those early days. I wanted to build PEOPLE. I wanted people to learn what I had learned. We built a great team, firing on all cylinders all the time. I was in the standard facility and there was a separate custom facility. We created processes. Processes are key.

Repeatability becomes profitability!

As I was going through this first leadership phase with Wisconsin Oven, Kodak came to us and asked that we develop an oven that was extremely customized. This was a challenge, but also an opportunity for growth. I worked with an engineer named Duane Lauersdorf to design the oven that achieved the results they needed. It was created mostly through trial and error.

Weld this.

And that.

Change the duct work.

Add air flow to the product.

Fix this.

Now that.

We were working sixteen-hour days and the deadline was coming up. We went back and forth until we finally scored a touchdown. It ended up being the catapult for Wisconsin Oven Corporation. We doubled the entire company's earnings with a single contract. We couldn't get proceeds from the patent yet, but were compensated in raise after raise after raise.

Now I was a leader, on a team that was leading, but somebody else was at the reins.

****

Henry Kubicki began Wisconsin Oven Corporation, but most people called him Hank. Hank didn't have a degree, but he was successful. He believed in promoting from within. For him, education was not the key to success in his organization; hard work was. He rewarded that hard work with opportunity. His philosophy was to create wealth for those who created it for him.

In every review I ever had with Hank, his words were, *"Build your team. Finish Clean."*

Years later, I still keep Hank's plaque on my wall. It reads:

My Goal Is:
> *To leave behind*
>> *a pool of talent*
>>> *with a vested interest*
> *Who will leave behind*
>> *a pool of talent*
>>> *with a vested interest.*

Henry Kubicki had all the right philosophies. He was set apart, though.

The philosophies Hank had weren't the ones he displayed in his leadership. Hank was formal, always in three-piece suits because he was proud of having earned them through his hard work. In fact, he put a dress code in place for the full office and leadership staff. Men would be in suits and ties of navy color, or pinstriped. Women needed to be in skirts and wear pantyhose. There was a real "us and them" vibe between leadership and workers.

Few ever got close to Hank beyond his executive team. Many of the employees thought of him as snobby, or even Prima Dona-like. He had a big car collection and big strings pulling at the workings of everything Wisconsin Oven had going on, even though he had long since pulled himself away from the men and women who were keeping it going.

Everything having to do with appearances had to be "just so." Suggestions were sometimes scoffed at. Hank had built a good company. What could others add? Obviously, if it weren't for the hard work of many, he wouldn't be able to live the life he had, though, so he selectively led, building just a few people over private lunches that often served to build even more walls between the leadership and the team.

Hank was measured and careful. While he began the company with a fellow professional, John Mitchell, John's sometimes wilder side was too much contrast for Hank and he bought him out as soon as he was able.

John went on to become a competitor. Hank then put in place a policy that there would be no hiring from any of our competitors. He wouldn't hear of it. The policy barred a lot of experienced talent from ever entering our doors. Hank feared anybody else's vision clouding his own. He even had an extremely strict zero nepotism policy. While it may sound decent on its face, in small communities where people know family or friends with great skill sets and work ethic, the policy severely limited our pool of available talented workers.

I was stuck in the middle at this time, not yet in a suit, but already part of the "us" team of managers and leaders. Things were starting to move fast.

- *Landing the Kodak contract energized Wisconsin Oven!*
- *Hank pushed the workers!*
- *The workload multiplied!*
- *Hank pushed the workers!*
- *I was offered the Vice President of Manufacturing position!*
- *Hank pushed the workers!*
- *I traded in my work clothes for a suit . . . hated that!*
- *Hank pushed the management!*
- *The floor was slammed!*
- *Hank pushed the workers!*
- *Nobody there had a life!*
- *Hank pushed the workers . . . and didn't tolerate any pushback*

Hank fired Bruce Champion.

Whoa.

Hold on, there.

Not Bruce.

It was heartbreaking. Right before Bruce Champion's termination, we had a lot of work on the shop floor and Bruce knew in his heart that he was done. He had been pushing back against Hank who he felt was pushing too hard against the team.

Bruce Champion *was* a champion of Wisconsin Oven Corporation!

Bruce wanted to build people; that's the very thing Hank's plaque claimed a desire to do. As the work piled on, and Hank attempted to control it all with a personal touch to only a small handful of suited personnel, everybody did more work and connected less with their working brothers and sisters. Bruce wanted to give a personal touch, coach others to work smarter *and* harder, as he'd done with me. He could reach just a handful of us in Hank's "just-so" world.

I realized how much greater this company could be if there was somebody who could touch many lives, rather than a few select people. What if everybody didn't have to be the smartest *and* the hardest working guy or gal, but instead worked together to be the smartest and hardest working team.

I needed to surround myself with talent and work together with them to accomplish great things. When Bruce had been here, under Hank, there were a select few chosen to lead. When he left, we realized that we needed a team to carry the victory in order to make it a lighter load.

When just a hero or two, instead of a team, have to do the carrying, even victory can be a burden.

Profile of a Coach: Bruce Champion

"Successful people are always looking for opportunities to help others."

~Brian Tracy

Bruce Champion went to the University of Wisconsin-Milwaukee, culminating in a degree in accounting. To some, it may seem boring or dull, but he embraced it, and truly enjoyed it. For ten years, he worked in accounting when—after working with a tax client who specialized in turnarounds—he was encouraged to move into the field of manufacturing so that he could understand operations. Lucky for me, that meant he would come to Wisconsin Oven Corporation.

Bruce will be the first to admit that most of what he did as a leader was instinctive. He learned what he needed to do but operated on his gut. Bruce was brought in to help reshape the organization to achieve continual improvement as opposed to the status quo . . . "and the most significant change that occurred," Bruce later shared, "was when we hired Dave Strand." It's humbling to hear.

When I came over to Wisconsin Oven, I was a young married guy and I had to initially take a pay cut. It was Bruce who always tried to give overtime to make up difference.

> *"When I hired him, I didn't know what a diamond in the rough he was. He was a down-to-earth, hard-working, young man. What we found in Dave was that he was willing to be a model employee. He worked hard, learned everything he could, paid attention, and desired excellence at whatever job he had to do."*

Bruce told me when I came on that he had three simple rules:

1. Show up every day
2. Show up on time every day
3. Have a pleasant attitude

"If you do those three things," he said, "We can find you opportunities for growth."

For a lot of people, Wisconsin Oven was just a job; they were doing it for the paycheck, not the pride. Not quality. What Bruce was really looking for in me was an attitude. I *wanted* success.

Because of that, Bruce was able to help me develop the aptitude to back up the attitude. He worked with me to become the best I could at each job from painting to designing. Jeff Kent was in the same mode. Bruce was available as a mentor to those who wanted to learn.

When I approached Bruce with the idea of bringing friends into the company—good people—and I wanted Wisconsin Oven to pay them more than we normally would have done, I learned that they trusted me. They hired my recommendations recognizing that I wanted to change the culture. Bruce realized that it was appropriate to work as team and want, **not just individual growth, but company success**.

Wisconsin Oven was doing well as small business. We were growing . . . making good money. Bruce was beginning to develop a management team.

> *"I remember the day when Dave quit and went over to our competition. Immediately, my gut said, 'we have a big problem because Dave is exactly the kind of guy we want!' Something was out of whack. Within a minute of my hearing he was quitting, I said 'Let's talk.' As I was spinning this through my head, I asked him 'What if I made you plant manager? Would you stay? I could place the current supervisor in a different opportunity.'"*

Obviously, I stayed, but so did my supervisor. Bruce really seemed to enjoy working with us and with other leaders that desired growth.

The founder of Zappos, Tony Hsieh, discusses in his book, *"Delivering Happiness,"* his belief that managers should socialize with their staffs. That was a very divergent view between Hank and Bruce. Bruce enjoyed an after work beer and game of pool with the guys. He also liked to help us to become motivated toward *professional* success, though. He used to hold all-volunteer sessions to listen to Brian Tracy motivational speaking sessions and I was one of the guys who was always there. Bruce loved sharing different success perspectives in these sessions and I was like a sponge for it.

All significant business is done based on the relationships we make. If you have a legitimate relationship with a supplier, if things go wrong, you work through it. Without relationship, you're in trouble. Without relationship, you're cut off at the knees.

Bruce wanted genuine relationship with genuine people.

Hank didn't relate to that "create relationship with everyone" type of attitude.

- Bruce would have fun and laugh with the team. Hank was so disciplined that he couldn't let his hair down.
- On the floor, Bruce wanted his coat off, his tie down, and his sleeves up. Hank did the opposite and suited up for the floor.
- Hank came across as *above* everybody and Bruce came across as *with* them.

The reality with Hank was that he needed someone who was willing to grow the business. Bruce just was at a point in my life when—right or wrong—he didn't NEED bigger. That's ultimately the reason why Bruce got fired.

Bruce exited gracefully but later shared that he was angry at Hank for a long time. He recognizes now that it was the right thing to do as a business and the business has flourished since. Hank was very respectful by noting that Bruce helped that business in many ways, but he was part of an era that wasn't moving forward with the company. At the time of his firing, it was very traumatic for him, as well as a lot of the team, but really? He just didn't fit, anymore.

"When I look at Wisconsin Oven now, I see all of the key people leading the organization: Jeff Kent, Dave Strand, and others. These guys were the ones I felt closest to. When I see the current success of Wisconsin Oven, I see my old core team. It's my proudest accomplishment from my Wisconsin Oven career."

"Love only grows by sharing. You can only have more for yourself by giving it away to others."

~Brian Tracy

****

During my difficult high school years, my grade problems nearly kept me from graduating. Girls were a distraction, money was always tight, and family life was stressful, but I loved football. Football was all I lived for at the time, but—in my sophomore year—I was declared ineligible to play because I was failing algebra, science, home economics, which I only signed up for to meet girls, and history. I think I was passing gym class.

This wonderful teacher and my football coach knew I was going through hard times, but they also knew that if I didn't have football, I'd be gone completely. I'd be lost and that wasn't okay with them.

They talked the science teacher into letting me do a twenty-page report at the end of the year to get me from an F to a D-. Hey, I passed. I didn't say I passed with flying colors. They weren't done with me yet. Next, they arranged for the home economics teacher to give me something for extra credit and I got to a D- with her, too.

The algebra teacher gave me an *incomplete* because, during the football season, I actually had skipped out every Friday due to being so sore. I had missed thirty-seven days of school that year and my dad never knew it. He went to work every morning and I would just stay in bed because my body

"Mentor"

Somebody that has compassion and genuine care for helping somebody without any interest and gain for themselves. To the mentor, true pleasure comes in helping others succeed.

~Dave's Definitions

had been so beaten up and drained that I just had Nothing. Left. To. Give.

Then, after my algebra teacher gave me that incomplete, she took me into her home all summer long. Mrs. Martha Bresler was her name and she mentored me and tutored me and I ended up with the hardest-earned C of my entire life. I was eligible for football, again. Mrs. Martha Bresler did so much for athletes and students over the years.

I lived for football. I loved the game. I loved my team, the East Troy Trojans.

That was absolutely a moment in my life where I realized the importance of helping people. It was really a game changer for me, not just because it got me back in the game, but it got me into the game of life.

For the first time, after Wisconsin Oven lost the mentor it had in Bruce Champion, I was going to have a chance to give back the way Martha Bresler gave back to me.

After Bruce left, I became the Vice President of Operations, over engineering, service, and manufacturing. We had separate vice presidents over sales and over finance. The vice presidents were all offered a seat on the board, sharing 20% of the company to Hank's 80% and Bruce, my mentor and friend, actually lent me the money for a property investment, which I later mortgaged to buy those shares.

It was 1996 and I was twenty-nine years old, surrounded by a board of directors who had, on average, four decades more experience than I had.

Over the next few years, the board kept growing. Hank opened up a middle-management buy-in. Pretty soon, we had twenty-five shareholders and no succession plan. People on the board actually began to pass away. Still, no plan was in place. Hank wanted all of these shareholders to turn into employee owners. Meanwhile, if they left the company, they had an unsecured note that stated they had five years to pay out any stock they had bought. We were creating debt and still there was no plan.

Lessons From The League Of Leaders!

We will always tend to fill our own expectations of ourselves.

~Brian Tracy

****

Hank got sick.

It was cancer.

It was coming on fast.

It was coming on strong.

You know those stories of working men who, on their death beds, regret having poured themselves into work instead of their loved ones? Sometimes, there are even miracles of their recoveries after such realizations. They give up their professional lives for more time, more rest, more family. They go on with their lives, however much of them they have left, basking in the life they sacrificed for all of those years that they spent building a company. Those stories have the power to collectively move us as people and professionals. The people in these stories make sense to us.

Hank wasn't that guy.

Wisconsin Oven *was* his family.

It was kind of awful when he finally wound up in hospice, shrunken and discolored. His company was his legacy, so he worked to shape it until his last breaths.

Hank called his leadership team to a meeting with him *in hospice* on the day before he died. He had a wife and kids, but sent out his family so that we could handle business. It was awkward for them and painful for us. Hank reiterated his "no nepotism" rule and made us all agree that his family would *not* be let in when he died.

Maybe part of Hank wanted his wife and children to be family for each other since the company had been his family. I'd like to believe that. Nonetheless, he wanted us to know that Wisconsin Oven was ours. It was horrible, but who argues with a man on his deathbed? It was, oddly enough, a power position.

"So help me God, when I die, do not let my family in," Hank had said. "This is your company."

Hank had asked me in a separate meeting earlier (which also took place in hospice) who I thought should be president when he died and I'd told him it should be the vice president of sales, because he'd been there longer. He asked me again. And again. I really felt it was the right decision. I had the skills, but the other guy had the tenure. I wasn't trying to step on any toes. Plus, I knew the guy and I could work for him, but I wasn't sure it would work the other way around.

So, there we all sat, bawling like grown men wouldn't care to admit, holding a leadership meeting over a dying man. It was horrible. Everything was scripted. He had an actual checklist of things we needed to cover.

- ✓ The Vice President of Finance was about to retire . . . in the less literal sense of the word . . . and Hank was dictating plans for his retirement party, while coughing and spitting fluids into a Dixie cup.
- ✓ And how were we doing on rewriting our mission statement?
- ✓ And how would we back-fill?
- ✓ And we were excused.

I had learned a lot from the man, much of which I didn't realize until after he was gone, but no goodbyes were spared. They weren't on the list.

It was the last time I ever saw him alive.

DID YOU KNOW?

IT TAKES THE HIDES OF 3,000 COWS TO MAKE ENOUGH FOOTBALLS FOR A FULL NFL SEASON.

ARE YOU CONSIDERING EVERY PART OF YOUR COSTS IN BUSINESS?

Injured Reserve

"Injury in general teaches you to appreciate every moment. I've had my share of injuries throughout my career. It's humbling. It gives you perspective. No matter how many times I've been hurt, I've learned from those injuries and I come back even more humble."

~Troy Polamalu

The new president played pretty well at-level and up, but below him, he wasn't so good. He kept the formal "us and them" policies of our previous president. Dress code was still suits for leaders. The team was still told what to do rather than brought in on the vision – the *why*.

He had a poor relationship with the human resources manager and women, in general. I kept my position as Vice President of Operations, but for the first two years of the new president's reign (new KING's reign); I had taken up the unaccredited role of damage control officer, running interference between our king and our people.

I served as this "Damage Control Officer" for two years, dealing with every office visit that began with "he did this," or "he did that." I was the face and voice of the people while they dealt with what sometimes seemed like outright bullying. He was trying to score with this team, but you can't throw touchdown passes with heavy fists!

Often, in leadership meetings, our president opened up by saying how much he wanted to weed the Wisconsin Oven garden. He always had a problem with somebody and his way of dealing with it was to put them down. Sometimes it was over something as elementary as talking on the plant floor. I would handle our King so that my team didn't have to.

****

Every winter, I was known for holding a big company party that I funded on my own. It was an annual ice fishing trip with a big jamboree, prizes, food, and some letdown time for the team. Everybody was welcome from the offices and the plants. I thought it was important to have an opportunity to bond from time to time outside of the walls of Wisconsin Oven. Almost everybody would show up.

On a Sunday during January of 2005, there was a snow storm during the annual event. I had hopped up onto my ATV to make a run to the house for supplies. Out of nowhere, my son's friend came through the weeds on another ATV and I got T-Boned. It was a party's-over-laid-out-not-going-anywhere-anytime-soon kind of crash.

I went to the emergency room and the local doctor was none too happy about having to come in and cast me up on a football Sunday. I was hooked up to a self-regulated morphine drip. I'd never been in so much pain in all my life. I literally maxed out the allotted medication; I lay on the release button all night long.

When the doctor came in the next day, he said, "I take it you have a low tolerance of pain."

"Get me out of here, NOW," I ordered. "I want a second opinion."

I was furious! I was sweating profusely. Couldn't he tell my pain was real? The doctor begrudgingly decided to take another look and began to poke my toe with a needle, except I couldn't feel it. Now, it was his turn to sweat. He'd screwed up . . . big time.

The cast was removed and they discovered that I had something called *Compartment Syndrome*. Essentially, it's an internal bleed within a muscle. Not only did I have to have emergency surgery, but I was told I'd have to walk with a cane the rest of my life and I may never again regain full mobility. *(Thankfully, as an aside, I disproved that theory.)*

I was out the use of my leg and Wisconsin Oven was out its unofficial damage control officer. I went home from the hospital, with my broken up leg, barely able to handle any thought more than healing. For one week, I didn't have to. Then, my leadership team visited.

Everybody . . . everybody except our president that was . . . showed up at my house. The well-wishes didn't fill much time before their real purpose was revealed.

"Dave," Jeff Kent, a (still-to-this-day) vice president, said, "We've all talked about it. You need to come back, or we're walking."

After a week of the president without me there to run interference, they couldn't handle it. He was a tyrant and this was a coup. If I didn't take over as president, they were quitting.

"I have to do it," I told my family. "They're my family, too. Besides, if they all walk, we still lose everything."

****

> ## *"Team" and "Family"*
>
> *There's really no difference between team and family. In order for a family to function well, it needs to operate like a team. In order for a team to function well, it needs to operate like a family.*
>
> *~Dave's Definitions*

****

The company entered a month-long soap opera as the board was pulled together. Many of them had been out of state, down in Florida. They had to be called back to take a vote to remove our current president. One of the board members was friends with the president. Except for him and our president, everybody voted for the change.

I felt awful sitting in the office while the guy I'd told Hank to put in the job got to hear all of the dirt from fellow leaders and team members. The sad thing was that we really had been friends before all of this. Sure. Our leadership styles were nothing alike, but we'd worked together for a long time and you can't help but bond with the people you share your daily life with.

I had to be the one to formally let him go. We hugged it out. We cried it out. We talked a few times after it happened, but it always felt terrible.

As a team, out of respect for the ousted leader, nobody spoke ill of him. In fact, as part of his departure, we agreed that there would be no slandering. We are part of a small community. It was an important decision.

Ironically, a few years later, he died in an ATV accident at the same lake where I'd had the ATV accident that injured my leg and ended in his termination.

****

No more guarantees.

I had received the ball.

It was time to take this team down the field toward victory.

On April 1, 2005, I was introduced as the new president of Wisconsin Oven Corporation.

My Timeline at Wisconsin Oven Corporation

top: sheet metal fabricator and painter; 1986-1988
bottom: (left) welder, assembler and field service; 1988-1992
(right) plant manager; 1992-1995

top: Vice President of Manufacturing; 1995-1997 VP of Operations; 1997-2005
bottom: Owner/President/CEO; 2005-2012. President/CEO; 2012-present

SECOND HALF

The exact words of the coaches in the Buffalo Bills' locker room were described by defensive coordinator Walt Corey as unrepeatable, but were – as he later shared – no different from the profanities the fans were shouting from the stands. Nose tackle Jeff Wright said that they, as a team, embarrassed themselves, embarrassed the coaches, and embarrassed the fans.

Despite Coach Mark Levy telling his team that they needed to find a reason to feel okay about themselves in the remaining thirty minutes of play, just under two minutes of play into the second half had the Oilers intercepting a pass for another touchdown. The score was 35-3, Houston.

"The lights are on here at Rich Stadium," a Houston radio announcer famously said. "They've been on since this morning. You could pretty much turn them out on the Bills right now."

Then, the wind literally shifted. It resulted in a squib kick, great field position, and a fifty-yard drive chipping away at the lead and putting Buffalo in the game, albeit barely, with a score of 35-10, Houston.

Onside kick! Christie added to his value again by recovering his own ball! Another drive and another touchdown. 35-17. Then, before the third quarter finished, a punt by Houston (their first of the game) and 7 more points for the Bills before most of the nation had known to tune back in. Buffalo wasn't done.

The fourth quarter began with an INTERCEPTION and, a few plays late, ANOTHER touchdown closing a near closeout to a four-point game: 35-31. The Bills were on fire! One touchdown later, Buffalo found itself in the lead for the first time: 38-35. Moon was back with a sixty-three yard drive, ending in a field goal; the "Lights Out Buffalo Bills" were miraculously going into overtime.

Christie got to be the hero one more time with a field goal to polish off— at a score of 41-38—the greatest comeback in American Football history!

A Championship Culture

Receiving The Ball

> *"First there are those who are winners, and know they are winners. Then there are the losers who know they are losers. Then there are those who are not winners, but don't know it. They're the ones for me. They never quit trying. They're the soul of our game."*
> **~Paul William "Bear" Bryant**

"You wanted him out," I told my vice presidents as we kicked off our new adventures. "Now, it's us. It's game time."

Growing up in Wisconsin, there are a few things that we expect the world to know about us. We drink Miller®, not Bud®. We have the best cheese in the world and our sausage isn't so bad, either. We hunt, fish, and use our land for some of the most sought after farm crops this country has to offer. We love the seven to nine months of cold, happily holding off on coats until it drops below 40 degrees Fahrenheit. We hit the beaches that appear alongside our more than 15,000 freshwater lakes—including two of the Great Lakes—when it gets to be about 60 degrees Fahrenheit. We wear Badger red, Brewers blue, and, from the end of August to (hopefully) February, proudly sport giant yellow, triangular, foam, Cheesehead hats atop our overly decked out Green Bay Packers green and gold.

If you ain't football, you ain't Wisconsin.

From 1992 to 2007, loving football as a Wisconsinite meant loving the NFL's all-time winningest quarterback, Brett Favre, Don Majkowski's successor who was also known as "The Gunslinger." In the fifteen seasons he spent at Lambeau field, he took the team to seven division championships, four NFC championships, and two Super Bowls, one of which the Packers won. Sundays in Wisconsin meant seeing 4's everywhere you went.

That's one hell of a tenure to have to follow. Most fans never wanted it to end. When Favre left, the reins would be handed over to a three-season backup who was completely unproven.

The thing is this; Favre had issues. He was known for being arrogant and demanding with his teammates and the team staff. He would butt heads with leadership and would often go his own way, separate from their unified vision if he thought he knew better than the coaches. Humility wasn't a part of his vocabulary. The year before his last with Green Bay, he even committed the ultimate sin by losing in a shutout to historic NFL rival, the Chicago Bears. Still, Favre was our guy. Why?

It was easy to overlook the flaws he had (minus that loss to the Bears, anyway) for something comfortable associated with great successes and memories. Wisconsin mourned as if we were experiencing a death when Favre retired. (*Of course, this was before a later betrayal of taking the helm with fellow central division team, Minnesota Vikings, after a return from retirement and a year as a New York Jet.*) What we didn't realize was that a new era was coming . . . the era of Aaron Rodgers.

We lacked a future vision.

Wisconsin Oven Corporation was at the end of our own era and it was about to get scary. Just like Green Bay Packer fans had to let go of Favre in order to embrace their new path, we were in need of some change. With me in the quarterback position, I had to be the one to lead that change. There's a well-known urban legend that deaths come in three.

Upon the death of our old company era, there would be three major areas changing:

- Product
- People
- Process

I kicked off change by getting back to basics. I looked around at the company that I had joined as a kid and started to recognize, for the first time, just how cluttered it had become. Wisconsin Oven did standard and custom industrial ovens and we did them well! We made them so well, in fact, that we had something to be proud of . . . a niche market as well as an international one.

No matter your business, you should never lose sight of your target demographic for your product or service.

The original owner had his hands in a number of non-industrial oven ventures along the way and he was always trying to eke out an extra penny here or there by using the successful base that he'd built at Wisconsin Oven as a launching pad for his entrepreneurialism.

At the time I took over, in addition to our core competencies, Wisconsin Oven was making two-cycle engines and motorized wheelbarrows, as well as distributing lab ovens. NONE of these lines were making us money. They were distractions. *Right* away, they *went* away. Nobody fought me too hard on product changes.

Changes in people are a different story. Some of the changes I had to make in people began to take place as early as when I was vice president.

I was the first from my high school class to get hired by Wisconsin Oven. As we began to take off as a company, I started to bring my friends in to be a part of the team. We were

---

New Leader Support

All eyes are on you!

The best coaches have a great support staff. It's just as important in business for leaders to have a team they can turn to when they need insights.

A great resource for such support is in professional business and executive coaching as found in TEC, Action Coach, Young Presidents' Organization (YPO), and other reputable sources.

From this support system, leaders can gain:

- *An Objective Counsel of Peers*
- *Great Resource of Speakers and Resources*
- *A Strong Professional Network*
- *The Collective Experience of Their Industry Colleagues*
- *Great Professional Development Recommendations*

It doesn't have to be lonely at the top!

growing so fast and, when painting at night one day, Bruce just asked me, "Do you know anyone looking for a job who can do 'this' or 'that'?"

Sure I did! I played football with a bunch of guys who could do the work. I mean, these guys were competitive! It would be great to have them at Wisconsin Oven Corporation. At one time, it was even a running joke that we should rename the plant, "The Class of '84."

By the time I became vice president, we'd all gotten into pretty successful positions within the company. I had two plant managers that I'd played ball with in high school in each of the two plants. I also had a great friend at the head of the service department. We were all close, but it wasn't 1984 anymore; we weren't classmates; and our company was modernizing, too.

Wisconsin Oven was going through the transition from the printing equipment that we were making for Kodak to something very different! We had been making a product that was very small and standard and now we needed to make these custom ovens that were complicated. This new line required more work, more procurement, more production, and all kinds of things that just didn't have processes yet. After our comfortable years, we needed a new kind of work ethic.

For everything to remain the same, everything must change.

This is true in business as much as in any field. You can't compete if you become stagnant and that's what was happening at Wisconsin Oven Corporation. At least, that's what was happening with our people. The products were changing but the people were lazy. They didn't want to do this new, customizing thing. They didn't want to start over.

One of my friends from high school had a hard time with change. The more we evolved, the more aggravated he got. He would buck the system and everyone under him was feeling intimidated. It bottled up growth for all of those beneath him.

My son and his were close and the unthinkable happened. He lost his own son to suicide. It was horrible. Because of the loss, I gave him time . . . a lot of time. We had to talk again and again about our new direction, but he just couldn't get on

> ### Lessons From The League Of Leaders!
>
> *"You can't build an adaptable organization without adaptable people--and individuals change only when they have to, or when they want to."*
>
> *~Gary Hamel, Founder of Strategos*

board. I gave him three years to heal and move forward with us, but he just bottled up, and went into his shell, stubborn and fighting the inevitable; fighting change.

I had to let him go. We cried it out. We hugged it out. Once again, my desk was witness to loss. He was one of my best friends. Then, I had to call in the rest of the Class of '84. These guys had played on the line together back in the day, so I knew it would be hard for them to accept that we'd lost a teammate. I owed them direct leadership and honesty. The plan was changing and I wanted them to be a part of the change, but the choice was theirs as to whether they would stick around in this new, redefined company.

One of my buddies chose to leave. It was on good terms, but the "people" shake-up was starting to be recognized by the rest of the company. My old teammates and I had been the three amigos. I wanted them to be a part of this team, too, but they needed to be willing to play by the new rules . . . the new playbook for our Aaron Rodgers era.

There was one more painful "people" change during our transitional growth. I had promoted an incredible talent from the floor to a service manager position. He was so valuable out on the floor as one of the most gifted electricians I ever knew. If anything ever went wrong, he was the go-to guy to fix it! I had a lesson to learn about putting the right people in the right positions on the line, though.

Just because somebody is good at a task, doesn't mean he or she is going to be good at directing others on that task.

Once I had promoted Chris to service manager, he was in the position of receiving all of the customer complaints. The role really wore him down and he carried that negativity to his team, instead of hope. He was a technician, not a manager. It was the equivalent of throwing a great kicker in as your quarterback!

I would ask, "How you doing today, Chris?" and the answer was always negative.

I couldn't break the downward cycle. It was tragic in a lot of ways. I had been the one to promote him beyond his level of competency. We were good friends. We'd go out for a beer together and play darts together when we were young. He had done an incredible job as an electrician and then I took him out of that role!

- Three ends to three product lines streamlined Wisconsin Oven.
- Three fires of three friends felt worse, by far, than losing Favre.
- The third big change was process.

Process would be the big change that would lead us to victory. Process was at the heart of championship culture. This was my game, now. I was quarterbacking in the second half of my career and the lessons learned at this time gave me a hard-earned touchdown to take forward toward victory.

3rd Quarter TOUCHDOWN

1. Steer clear of profanity.

2. You can't throw a touchdown with a heavy fist!

3. Be direct and sincere.

4. Inspire hope.

5. Don't ask what you aren't willing to do, yourself.

6. Recognize unhealthy competition.

7. <u>Be a friend</u>: letting somebody go doesn't have to mean letting them down.

~Leadership Lessons As You Quarterback Your Team

DID YOU KNOW?

AN INCOMPLETE FORWARD PASS IN FOOTBALL USED TO EARN A TEAM A 15-YARD PENALTY.

MAKE SURE YOU PUT YOUR PLAN IN PLACE BEFORE YOUR PLAY IF YOU DON'T WANT TO LOSE GROUND!

The New Playbook

"No one gives a crap about what you did last week. This league is about what have you done for me now. That's the NFL. It's also our culture. So you keep working hard because that's the biggest truth about football."
~Andrew Luck

Culture is the heartbeat of any and all businesses and teams. It's not the product, the building, or the strategy; it's the people. The people have to have shared vision, strong leadership, and the ability to work as a team. That team has to have developed strength relating to one another just by being together. Leadership and team members must have instilled confidence in one another that they are there for one another.

When I thought about what I define as "culture" and "teamwork," I was easily able to see that culture was the very thing was hurting Wisconsin Oven's ability to grow and score big as an industry competitor. Teamwork, by the way, wasn't a part of the culture at all. I took over the company at its lowest point, having recently lost the major Kodak account. The world had gone digital and Kodak didn't. If we weren't careful, we would be left behind, too, like all of the other relics of the pre-computerized age. The guys and gals of my company were family to me. It was vital that we all succeed. We needed to change.

That vision Hank had insisted from his deathbed that we write did ultimately get finished. "Wisconsin Oven Corporation was built on a tradition of integrity, quality, and service . . ." Yadda, yadda, yadda. Using buzz words wasn't what we were about! With a vision like that, we could be anything from a financial company, to a restaurant! We needed something that was going to champion the way for our new growth. Early in my presidency, we launched the Wisconsin Oven Corporation (W.O.C.) mission statement that launched our work of champions.

AT

Wisconsin Oven Corporation

OUR

Work Of Champions

Will Outperform Competition

AND

Win Our Customers

With Ongoing Commitment

Some talk the talk

We WOC the walk!

Everybody in the company can recite this mission statement, but I wanted them to live it, too. This was the clear vision that I had to present to the company. I had been continuing in the professional development traditions that Bruce Champion began with me years ago and Jim Collin's book, *"Good To Great,"* was a foundational inspiration for me. The first thing I needed to get down was VISION.

"Why *can't* we be the best oven company in the world?" I asked them.

All we had to do was beat our chests on our customer service. We needed to see through the vision that we were going to be the greatest. Big. Simple. Easy.

"Let's be the best. **What's holding us back?** This is the work of champions; the vision; let's WOC the walk."

Access the Electronic Resource Hub:

Scan the QR code to see more about defining a championship culture

Our vision became our ongoing commitment and, with heart, we were going to get there. First, though, I had to address a question: "What *was* holding us back?" When it comes to changing culture, leaders face an uphill battle. Wisconsin Oven Corporation was the Buffalo Bills at the halftime of their comeback.

- We were defeated by our losses.
- Our own people stopped believing in us.
- Our outcome was being decided and announced to the world.
- In no time, it seemed, we could be "lights out."

It's true that we had some leadership issues that got us to this point in the game, but that was in our past. It was time that we recognized the kinds of penalties that would hold us back from scoring again in the future . . . and cut them out of our mentality, our actions, and our operations.

Sometimes, before you can be a coach, you have to be your team's referee.

PERSONAL FOULS!

1. *Negativity!*

2. *Hero complex!*

3. *Calling your own plays!*

4. *Not communicating!*

5. *Not documenting the process!*

6. *Lack of accountability!*

7. *Not being on board with the goal!*

8. *Poorly managed conflict!*

9. *Complacency!*

10. *Stubbornness!*

11. *Entitlement!*

12. *Disregarding the importance of health!*

13. *Lack of appreciation for life balance!*

14. *Ignoring safety in the workplace!*

15. *Not having your team's back!*

~15 Penalties That Can Keep Your Team From Scoring Big

Jim Collins *"Good To Great"* tells us to start with who. I needed to make sure I had comeback players and I needed to make sure they were working in the positions that would benefit the whole team.

Right position on the line . . .

The right position on the line depends on the kinds of plays your team needs to make and, in this time of a new playbook, we had to deal with three types of players.

1) The Complacent:

Before the crash of Kodak, we had a lot of high level performers, but when the game plan changed and we had to function at a different level, it was obvious that some weren't even willing to be on the line at all because it was going to be harder – not a guaranteed win. These were guys who wanted to keep the compensation they had been earning, but without the new responsibilities of ownership and accountability.

2) The Overwhelmed:

We had other people who had promoted beyond their levels of competence. Sometimes it worked; sometimes it didn't. They were good at what they did from a technical standpoint, but they couldn't handle the responsibility of leading others and were in way over their heads.

3) The Specifically Skilled:

We had, for example, an engineer that we had moved into engineering from shop floor and he took general classes, so we thought he had experience. He'd taken CAD classes and we assumed he would be fine. But, he made a lot of mistakes to the point that we had to move him back into production from leadership. It was a *lead* production role, but he went from being white collar back to being blue collar.

With each of these player types, it was my job, with the help of my leadership team, to get them placed where they could personally excel in a way that would be beneficial to the whole company mission. We followed some simple steps to make sure we could address each type of team member in the most effective way for success:

1) Scouting:

Identify each of the team members early in the game to discover their specific competencies and their potential ability to change positions on the line.

2) Player Coaching:

Work with the team member to try to get them to effectively serving in his or her current position.

3) Head Coaching:

For great players, consider offering a lateral move to a right position from a wrong position.

"Hey, we need you to make a move. Your current role isn't working out."

Good coaches should be able to highlight the positive value of a position change. It's not about having conversations about what was done on first down, way back in the rearview mirror; it's about moving the team forward on third and long, where we were playing from that day. We compensated those who had to make those lateral moves according to tenure rather than position. By implementing that sort of payment plan, we knew that the guys who couldn't make the move couldn't do so because of ego as opposed to need.

Four Chances To Move The Chains

When I was Vice President of Manufacturing, I found myself wanting to be a mentor-style leader, like Bruce had been for me. If the player doesn't want to be mentored, though, the coach sometimes has to make hard decisions.

There was one guy I brought in from high school, when I had been with the company for six years. We played ball together in school. He came in and did well, starting in the shop, then working in the service department, and eventually travelling to perform installation and service on the equipment. When there wasn't enough work to send him out to the field, he'd come back to the shop, but he'd gotten sloppy.

First Down: One day, his actions resulted in a high-voltage shock that nearly electrocuted him. He never would have done it if he hadn't violated a safety policy and I was upset, but I was also grateful he was alright. "You could have killed yourself!" I remember saying. "Thank God you're alive. NOW, I hope you can get your act together."

Second Down: We put him back into field service. We gave cash advances back in those days and the workers would turn in receipts. His first time back, he was short $400 on his expense report. He said he messed up and we allowed it. (That number would slowly climb to the point where he owed $2000.00 to the company.)

Third and Long: We had a big customer for a big job out in California and he didn't show up. He went completely AWOL. He ended up being gone for two weeks and somebody else was sent out there.

Hail Mary On Fourth: Shortly after his disappearance, the whispers began that this guy had gotten himself caught up in a cocaine habit and he'd been seen in town. I went to his apartment and knocked and knocked and knocked. I was worried. All of his curtains were drawn. I called the local police. He was alive . . . but a mess. I drove him to rehab myself and told him to get cleaned up so we could move on.

He only stayed clean for a month and, ultimately, we had to let him go.

4) Refereeing:

Sometimes, you have to kick a guy out of the game.

If, after identifying team needs and team players, after working with the team, and after offering positions that fit both the player and the team best, the change is either not accepted or not working.

"Either you're willing to change positions on the line, or the team moves forward without you."

Every single time we had a player exit during that transitional time period—during our cultural change—more positive came out of it than negative. I saw my most competent managers at work and, together, we were able to see how much our right players were being held back by our

Contributing Team Member

Contributes individual capabilities to the achievement of group objectives and works effectively with others in a group setting.

Competent Manager

Organizes people and resources toward the effective and efficient pursuit of predetermined objectives.

wrong ones. It was as if our team just couldn't wait for the block to be removed. They needed to grow and go at full pace. It was like watching Aaron Rodgers take over after Favre; we catapulted to the next level!

As for our over-promoted engineer, he spent more time in production and took more classes. He worked his way back up. We knew he'd been there before, but his mistakes had always been good-hearted mistakes. He would come in, work long hours, and do what needed to be done. He had the heart. This guy really cared and now he also had the ability and experience to get it on paper and in blueprints.

Through hard work and focus, he had a new opportunity. We told him it was time to move forward. Today, he's a senior engineer and he has had to do project management. His move back to production was the equivalent of training camp; he went through it and became one of our best contributing team members.

****

Dave on Hiring

Putting people in the right position on the line starts in the hiring process and is necessary from those second and third shift painters all the way up to vice president level positions.

I recently interviewed five people for an executive level management position. It was kind of neat because they each had a different style. It was like the flavor of the day.

- *I met one person who had worked his way up into a management position because of technical skills, but he wasn't personable.*
- *Another had all of the credentials. I could hear all about process, safety, and industry buzz words, but the personality wasn't right.*
- *Some came in stuffy and robotic, trying to oversell themselves.*

A lot of times you get these long resumes of qualifications, but when you take them to the pros and really put him in the field, statistics won't carry you to a victory. You have to be a leader. I want to just have an open conversation in an interview and talk about your style. How do you treat people? How do you reward wins? How do you define success?

As to the success question, it's not about profitability, by the way. Profitability is just the inevitable result of good processes. And good processes are the result of taking care of good people. The guys who had that answer? The people person? That was the right guy for the job.

The reason I still talk about people after we've moved onto process is that there are processes *around* those people. It's also the people who will be performing all of the processes of an organization. The flea-flicker only worked when there was somebody quick enough to put it in play.

Jim Collins describes quality people in a compact and easy-to understand way in his book, "Good to Great." He talks about the dual role of professional will and personal humility:

Professional will . . .

1) Creates superb results, a clear catalyst in the transition from good to great.
2) Demonstrates an unwavering resolve to do whatever must be done to produce the best long-term results, no matter how difficult.
3) Sets the standard of building an enduring great company; will settle for nothing less.
4) Looks in the mirror, not out the window, to apportion responsibility for poor results, never blaming other people, external factors, or bad luck.

Wisconsin Oven hired this young kid that had nothing more than heart named Dave Strand. Once somebody new learned the basics and went on to formal training for welding, someone had to train the new employee how to build ovens. That's where Larry Van Dan came in.

Larry was the perfect father and grandfather. He possessed this incredible passion for the company and was blessed with the gift of patience beyond belief. I can tell you that I was lucky to have Larry as my own trainer early in my Wisconsin Oven career.

Like an athlete rookie that has just been drafted into the NFL, no matter the talent and heart, you need to have the smarts and dedication to learn the plays. If you can't understand the playbook, you will not be able to execute the plays and help the team win.

Larry was the company man before me that would always do WHATEVER IT TOOK to get the result for our customers. He was the one who would be found opening the door for me at four o'clock in the morning, and walking out the door with me at eight o'clock at night, if that is what was needed that day.

We didn't have modern tools. We worked too hard, lifted too much, inhaled too much paint, and washed the day off of our beaten up bodies with paint thinner.

Larry was a player coach who led by the only example he knew.

When Larry was dealt the task of training this new kid – a wild mustang, he needed to figure out how to break him in. Larry trained me patiently on process.

In the end I learned process and I probably taught him a little more patience!

I then had the ability to read blueprints, weld, and maintain a high energy that was almost dangerous. I would learn that I needed to walk before I ran. There were many articulate steps that were required throughout the process of building a quality product that forced me to slow down and *keep learning*.

I made many mistakes, and sometimes I thought that I was disappointing Larry and may even get fired. It was never the case at all! Every time I would fall down and made a mistake, he would pick me up, dust me off, and reinstall confidence in me.

Life is full of opportunity. Hard work, passion, and perseverance are often the credit for success in life. Hell, it's where I put a lot of credit. However, I'm also a firm believer that a little luck and in being in the right place at the right time, too. If you have the right people in your life, they can catapult you to success. I equally believe that if you give life and everyone in it all that you have to give, those blessings show up on your doorstep one day as repayment. I was blessed that Larry was assigned to me. He had an incredible amount of stamina and unwavering dedication to the company's success, and a desire to teach everyone what he had learned over the years.

Larry soon had the pleasure of watching me become the most successful understudy he had ever trained. In the end I ended up being his boss. Instead of any kind of resentment, that actually made Larry become an even more passionate trainer. I'd go as far to say he's the most passionate trainer Wisconsin Oven has ever had the pleasure of employing!

Larry worked until his legs and back literally couldn't hold out any longer. After retirement and many surgeries, Larry would often come back like Favre and give it one more season. After five years of retirements and returns, Larry finally hung it up after twenty-six years of employment with Wisconsin Oven Corporation.

After true retirement and major health issues, one of his greatest thrills was to go for a drive to the plant and come pay the man in the corner office, his once-trainee, a visit. No matter how busy I was, no matter how many meetings I had scheduled, when the receptionist paged me to tell me Larry was in the house for a visit, my schedule changed. We would spend at least an hour, sometimes two, reminiscing about the days that he and that wild mustang would gallop through the field of challenges that eventually led to both of our greatest accomplishments in life!

Larry passed away on April 24th, 2014 at the age of 79. About one month before his passing, Steve Bertschinger, Jeff Kent, and I, (all great beneficiaries of his training, passion and patience) paid Larry a visit at his home over lunch. It was nearly a two hour visit. That day we witnessed a man who was near the end of his path and was suffering from every ailment you could imagine. Yet, he seemed to surge with new energy during our visit.

We replayed memories, great accomplishments, and funny stories. Before we left he gave me a box filled with every promotional Wisconsin Oven trinket ever released. He saved every one of them. Combs, pens, golf balls, photos, articles, knives. You name it; he had it in that box. As we left that cloudy day in mid-March, we looked back at the door and witnessed his smile and a last wave goodbye.

We waved back with tears in our eyes and said "Thank you Larry, we will see you again soon someday".

Rest in peace my dear friend, Larry Van Dan, you were the greatest warrior of professional will I ever have had the pleasure working with side-by-side! Thank you; I will never forget you!

Personal humility . . .

1) Demonstrates a compelling modesty, shunning public adulation; never boastful.
2) Acts with quiet, calm determination; relies principally on inspired standards, not inspiring charisma, to motivate.
3) Channels ambition into the company, not the self; sets up successors for even greater success in the next generation.
4) Looks out the window, not in the mirror, to apportion credit for the success of the company-to other people, external factors, and good luck.

Mike Grande is a guy who left Wisconsin Oven in 2009 for one of our competitors. His head wasn't in the game at the time that he left. We had been going through some custom projects that went bad. Mistakes were made on some high-risk projects that were underpriced. He had a lot of guys he was in charge of on the custom engineering team and they're all pretty close. They suffered when he made mistakes. The company suffered.

At our competitor, Mike became a Vice President. There were rumors that the company was about to go under and I immediately thought of Mike. This was a guy who had done some great things for us. He just needed to understand risk mitigation. I wanted to bring his skill set back, but couldn't trust bringing him back into leadership right away.

I brought Mike to the custom applications engineering team and asked them, "Hey guys, are you open to having Mike back?"

They wanted him to be a part of the team. He used to be their boss and, after that, a vice president with our competitor, but now he's their peer and he is hitting it out of the park every single day. Mike moved from an office to a cubicle and he loves his job as a senior applications sales engineer.

He is humble and helpful.

He brought back in-depth understanding of pricing.

He's gained experience.

He's polished.

I don't know what the decision to return to Wisconsin Oven in a different capacity looked like for Mike, but I know he exemplifies personal humility constantly as a team member and it takes a great leader to make such an incredible transition with grace and success.

Beyond professional will and personal humility, there are some traits, according to Jim Collins, that make the difference between good and great. He calls these traits out according to different levels of leadership with the "great" leaders being "Level 5 Leaders."

Level 5 Leaders . . .

Highly Capable Individual

- Talent
- Knowledge
- Skills
- Good Work Ethic

Contributing Team Member

- Individual Abilities
- Group Objectives

Competent Manager

- Organizational Skills
- Group Objectives

Effective Leader

- Communicates Vision
- Generates Commitment

Level 5 Executive

- Encompasses Professional Will
- Demonstrates Personal Humility
- Works for Company *Greatness*

I knew that if I wanted quality people at the team level, they needed to be led by quality people at the managerial level. I had Bruce Champion and it was necessary for me to put champions in place for all of the highly capable individuals and contributing team members that were a part of the Wisconsin Oven Corporation.

> ## *"Leader"*
>
> *It's somebody that is born versus built, but can be developed through self-confidence. Leaders make their companies their home teams. With every win, and every loss, they learn something. They know their teams, their audiences, and the motivators of those who can lead them to success.*

DID YOU KNOW?

PRIOR TO 1974, THE FIELD GOAL POSTS WERE FLUSH WITH THE BACK OF THE END ZONE AND ACTUALLY PROTRUDING INTO THE TOUCHDOWN AREA MAKING CENTER PASSES AWKWARD AND DIFFICULT.

DON'T STAND IN THE WAY OF YOUR OWN FORWARD PROGRESS!

Profile of a Team Captain

Believe it or not, Jeff Kent and I met in kindergarten. We weren't going to be in the same school for the elementary grades, but—at that time—all kindergarteners in the community went to the same school together. So, we'd have a year together. We were best friends as much as kindergarten-aged boys can be best friends. In fact, Jeff's mom still picks on him, today, over the fact that he cried at the end of the year when he realized we wouldn't still be classmates the next year.

We were reunited in the sixth grade and we've been friends ever since. We were wrestling partners in school. I was a nose guard on the football team to Jeff's running back. The two of us were from pretty poor families, so we shared those struggles, together. We also learned (decided) that hard work was going to be needed to get by in life. We both had a desire to be more financially stable than we were able to be as kids. For the most part, though, we were just typical young friends; I had no idea how we would continue to impact one another's lives for decades to come.

Because I got married and started having kids right out of high school and Jeff went away to college at The University of Wisconsin – Whitewater, we went our separate ways for a few years. There was no bad blood; we each knew what the other was up to, but we were just busy living very different lives and not hanging out together.

I started at Wisconsin Oven in July of the year Jeff had just finished college. He was taking time off to figure out his next steps and, the following May, he ended up returning home to Wisconsin Oven seeking work. He didn't even know I was working there.

When Jeff was on a tour of the plant before he began working there, I was on a creeper underneath a draw batch furnace giving it an acid-wash. That's when I felt a nudge against my foot. I slid out and was looking back at Jeff's ugly mug! I remember pulling my protective mask off and it was as if no time had passed between the two of us. Jeff would come spend time with the family, have dinner with us, play with the kids, and even pull out some Nintendo like we were still kids.

Jeff has his own story of when I nearly left for one of our competitors. Apparently, it's a real defining moment in Wisconsin Oven History. When upper management started to see me as a leader, my peers did, too.

The unique thing about Wisconsin Oven is that employees are promoted based on ability to work, not just their pedigrees, educations, or even their tenures. Hard work moves you up the ladder. Like me, Jeff bounced around a few departments before he became the sales manager in 1994. Because I was in production and Jeff was in sales, I didn't actually become his "boss" until I was president.

Jeff is a peer, but he understood that the health of Wisconsin Oven Corporation had to come before relationships. However, because of strong relationships, Wisconsin Oven Corporation was destined to succeed. Employees are family, but Jeff got the fact that we couldn't lose sight of the greater good and all of the families that would be better off when the whole company did well.

Losing our friends from the Class of 1984 to terminations was hard, but we worked with anybody that was willing to be coached. Living near one another, Jeff and I used to go for hour and a half long walks to discuss our mentorship programs for employees' improvement. We wanted to be able to wake up, look in a mirror, and know that we'd provided every possible chance to succeed to our team . . . even our old high school team.

Even with the break-up of the old high school crew, Jeff and I recognize that there was a nucleus of implicit trust that might not have otherwise been built without those guys. We'd all known one another for so long and, going back to sports, we understood the definition of being teammates; there's a need for selflessness. When we let down the company, it was more than letting down a boss; it was letting down a friend . . . a member of our extended family.

When I was injured and the leadership team came to my home, Jeff led that effort. I could tell he was serious. He definitely would have walked. The president at the time had been trying to play Jeff and me against each other. He'd say half-truths to see if he could break our trust between one another. Jeff was at a point in his career where he was not happy. He thought about quitting and was very angry that the vision Hank had on his office plaque and what Wisconsin Oven had become were two vastly different things.

He said, "Dave, are we going to let the current president do this to the company, because I'm done. Are you going to make a move?"

Jeff wasn't interested in taking over. He wanted my experience including the leadership, mentorship, and trust that I'd received from Hank and Bruce. Jeff wanted the value of knowing Hank's goals and thoughts and he trusted me to do a good job. It fueled the fire within me to realize that he and I were on the same page.

There was a moment of change that sort of marked the cultural future of Wisconsin Oven that took place after I became president. Jeff was my team captain and, together, we talked about getting our people in right positions on the line. The meeting was full of gut-wrenching, soul-searching questions: *Who truly wants to be on the team? Who is willing to change positions to be successful?* This was serious. We needed major changes and I needed the major enthusiasm of people like Jeff. We realized that not everybody was going to make the final cut for the team, but those that did would be on our CHAMPIONSHIP TEAM.

I'm blessed to have Jeff as one of those team captains. His standards are logical:

- Lead by example
- Provide the critical support to those on your teams; the leadership triangle is often and upward pyramid; but we like the pyramid upside down with the president holding up the executive team who—in turn—holds up the team players
- Answer questions
- Provide tools
- Have an open door policy
- Be a positive energy cheerleader for the team
- Be purpose-driven
- Maintain a relationship connection to as many team members as possible

Business is an opportunity for continuous improvement. Every single day has opportunities to improve. Jeff and I look at Wisconsin Oven the same way; there's always a chance to do better. We continue to try to improve quality, drive prices down, and encourage a family environment in company and community. We'll continue to grow as a company.

As friends, I don't question our relationship. We've been together so long, trusting each other so much. Over and over again, we are on the same page. We have become similar in knowing the goals and how to get there. We sometimes have different paths, but we all know the goal: A Championship Culture.

top: Jeff and me at my 17th birthday party, 1983
bottom: Celebrating Wisconsin Oven Corp Standard Division's 25th
anniversary, 2003; (left to right) Chuck Heckman, me, and Jeff

With players on the right positions on the line and great leaders to coach them, it was time to start becoming a cohesive unit . . . a TEAM.

Working as a team is broken down into two basic areas: breaking down the silos between divisions and celebrating wins together. By succeeding in these two areas, you succeed in building a championship culture.

How many times in business do we have redundancy because of a lack of communication between the different areas of business? You'll find on Google searches that a lot of research has been done on this subject in Europe, but it's been mostly neglected in the United States. On the level of federal government, redundancy is estimated to cost in the tens of billions; that's billions with a "b." Most redundancies occur as a result of one group not knowing or realizing what another group is doing. They are each operating within their own silos.

Effective leaders need to break silos down in order to get everybody working on the same goals without stepping on one another's toes. This is where a strong value stream comes in. We spend so much time as business leaders focusing on serving our customers that we often neglect the importance of serving one another. We are our own *internal* customers.

Dave on Conflict Resolution

Anytime you have more than one person in a situation, the odds are you'll have more than one opinion on how to handle that situation.

If you don't learn as a leader how to manage conflict resolution early on, you will end up having to face bigger, more difficult, and more costly issues as time allows those small problems to fester.

I remember having two employees who worked on the same shop floor together, but each with different goals. They had a negatively competitive approach to those end goals, wanting to hold one another back rather than lift one another up.

They were both a little on the abrasive side and had a tendency toward negative attitudes to the point that they had received both verbal and written reprimands from their floor supervisors.

Both employees were well-skilled and well-trained. They got results, so they were worth working with as a player coach to see if we could make them work for the company.

That's when I decided to "marry" the two. They needed to become family because that was the concept that made our whole team—our whole company—work. They were going to play together as a team

If EITHER one of them won by meeting a goal, it counted as a win for both of them; if EITHER one of them lost by missing a goal, it was a loss for both of them; and if I had to fire one, I'd be firing both.

One of the two employees stepped up his game and worked hard to make successes for both. The other was bitter about the arrangement and eventually left the company. Immediately, the employee who had made changes was worried for his own employment. He had screwed up in the past and was prepared to pay the consequences.

The great thing about this story is that there were no other consequences to be paid. Why would I terminate the employment of a team member who had learned to be a team player? Not only did he stay, but he was grateful for the opportunity; he turned over a new leaf in his attitude and is now our longest tenured worker at Wisconsin Oven Corporation.

4th Quarter TOUCHDOWN

1. Be kind. My mother-in-law, Mary Flath, says it best: "If you start out mean, it's hard to go back to kindness, but if you start out kind, you still have the option to be tough when the situation calls for it without losing your kindness."

2. Know when to use the sugar and when to use the stick. One mistake may need a gentle approach, but repeated inability to execute on assignments could call for a more disciplined and clear explanation of expectations.

3. Reward good performance — celebrate every victory no matter how big or small.

4. Provide a clear vision with a path to victory, a playbook of processes, and built-in necessary mentoring along the way.

5. Nothing lasts forever. Don't get complacent; you'll need to reinvent your playbook more than once based on changing technology, changing clients, the economy, and more. Don't rest on your laurels.

6. Be real. Be comfortable. Be yourself. Be authentic. When you're finally good with who you are, you'll be able to lead without anxiety and with authority.

7. Be a friend. You want your team to see you as family so that you can work together like one.

~Leadership Lessons As You Coach Your Team

When it was time to change the Wisconsin Oven playbook, I sat down with my team, a stack of post-its and a blank wall. We needed to figure out the HOW of serving our customers and it ultimately led directly to the WHO of our internal customers.

Who is the customer?

How do we get the order?

Once we get the order, where does it go?

None of these questions were actually defined. We had tribal knowledge, but no actual processes. We needed to hash out the things that we thought we knew to develop processes that would lead to efficient, on-time delivery without redundancy.

Value streaming is necessary to efficiently run teams and organizations.

An example of our process included a focus on the path of a sale from our external customer through all of our internal departments and back out to the external customer.

- From an external customer (lead), the order goes to sales.
- After the sale, the needs are sent to engineering.
- After engineering's design, they work with procurement.
- Once needs are procured, the order goes to production.
- A finished product gets inspected by quality.
- Quality department approves a product for shipment.
- Shipping gets the product to the eternal customer.

Our value stream was the first part of our people process. Before getting into the second people process, it's important to address the other processes that needed to be in place for a championship culture. It was these processes that a now cohesive team would be in charge of seeing through.

****

To create processes, it was necessary to implement a process.
1) What's the question?
2) What's the answer?
3) How do we achieve the answer?

Administration . . .

Question – What are all of the required documents for the growth of our business?

Answer – Each department (sales, engineering, procurement, production, quality, shipment) has documentation.

How – Communicate with each department to ask about their steps. Create lists for necessary documentation. Eliminate redundancy by assigning overlap to single departments and removing those from other departments.

Question – How do we instill discipline in administrative processes?

Answer – Communicate the efficiency to the team to bring them on-board with the vision.

How – This is on leadership! Maintain a positive tone and show the advantages of working together.

Question – How do we document changes as they occur and communicate them for understanding among all employees?

Answer – Make sure there is team buy-in for changes.

How – Discuss changes before the mandate in order to guide toward the best decisions for the company.

Question – How do we standardize and modernize communication between our many facilities?

Answer – Make sure the Value Stream (the internal customer route) is available to all employees.

How – Have an open door policy with leadership and no more "us and them" teams. If the management is on the same team with the workers, the workers will be on the same team with one another.

Question – What is the routine schedule for communication? (Daily? Weekly? Monthly? Quarterly?)

Answer – All of the above!

How – Hold daily or weekly tool box talks, weekly staff meetings, monthly company meetings, and quarterly board meetings. One of our foremen brought "box talks" to our floors. What our guys in the shop do is, at least weekly, they get together around the tool box to discuss things that pertain specifically to their shop. It might be process, but it might also be about other things. These are our blue collar meetings led by shop supervisors. It's a safe, comfortable environment without big group (or big leadership) pressure.

Administration processes are all about reviewing the playbook and making sure that everybody on the team knows the rules of the game.

Operations . . .

Question –What is our marketing strategy; define and discover.

Answer – Do what we do best and tell the world.

How –The internet is a wonderful thing; invest big!

Question–How do we leverage modern technology for all of the processes we need?

Answer – Be in the know and invest in what "fits" your company.

How –Rely on the younger talent in the organization, they are the "tech geeks" (and proud of it). In addition, younger generations, if not challenged and able to work with their mind and all of the things that are related to technology, they can move on and get bored. The thirty year vet who is a third generation employee of a factory? Those guys don't exist, anymore. If you challenge and take advantage of the knowledge of your young workers, you will not only leverage technology, you will decrease turnover and retain your people.

Question – How do we utilize what we've learned in the past and marry it to our engineering in order to produce at lowest cost?

Answer – Standardize everything possible!

How –Assign a Saturday morning breakfast club committee to standardization; otherwise there is no time and you'll find yourself reinventing the wheel every day.

Question – How do we create processes for long-lead, custom items?

Answer – New projects need a specialized kick-off meeting!

How –Have a huddle before every custom job, identify those long lead items and soon a process for pre-orders will be developed.

Question – How do we streamline procurement to production?

Answer – Ensure standardization on all standard products and kick-off meetings on all custom products.

How –Your head of procurement needs to participate in all production meetings and, between all of your departments, ensure that you have: communication, communication, and communication!

Question – How do we streamline production in a lean fashion?
Answer – Implement a formal lean manufacturing program.
How –Hire a proven consultant and read *"The Toyota Way"* by Dr. Jeffrey K. Liker.

> ### Lessons From The League Of Leaders!
>
> *"Every team member has the responsibility to stop the line every time they see something that is out of standard. That's how we put the responsibility for quality in the hands of our team members."*
>
> *~Dr. Jeffrey K. Liker, "The Toyota Way: 14 Management Principles from the World's Greatest Manufacturer"*

Question – How do we maintain safety, particularly with new, large equipment and new regulatory environment?
Answer – I hate to say it, but—when it comes to safety—be anal; you absolutely must support safety from the top down.
How –Create a safety sleuth program that includes all employees and rewards them for their findings of all hazards.

Question – How do we build in quality control procedures throughout the production?

Answer – Create a quality control department that documents every critical quality standard from inception of order to its shipment. *Quality is not just in the product it is in the process.*

How – You may need a separate department to be the "referee." This department should have the authority to stand in front of the loading dock no matter what! In the long run, shoddy quality on an order will cost you far more than a delay on an order.

Question – How do we reposition ourselves from a retailer to a consultant – industry expert - to our clients?

Answer – Leverage experience, and WOW (Wisconsin Oven Way) factor.

> *"In business there are only a few ways to differentiate yourself from the competition. It is your people that can create the real difference, who can create the WOW experience. And the WOW experience is something that causes your customer to feel a positive tingle, to want to come back and back and back to you. At Wisconsin Oven our goal is to provide our customers with outstanding customer service. We want all our customers to experience the WOW factor."*
> **~Wisconsin Oven Corporation**

How –Get your superstars in front of customers whenever possible. Get your customers to your facilities to witness the pride and quality byproduct of our team.

Question – How do we make service relational with preventative maintenance and regular communication?

Answer – Make your "service force" a part of your sales force.

How – Get inside and develop aftermarket opportunities. Your service team can be your best sales people. They know the product inside and out and they have an ear to the ground with people deep in the organization.

When it comes to operations, it's like a 99-yard scoring drive. Every single department has to hand off smoothly to the next department, inch-by-inch, step-by-step, one yard at a time, all the way to the goal line. Operational processes are at the heart of a value stream.

Finance . . .

Question – How do we communicate our goals to our employees?

Answer – Provide a scoreboard. And, OVER communicate it!

How –A good finance department can boil down the numbers to smaller, measurable statistics to make them real and comprehensible for employees. Instead of looking at the huge numbers, measure what is important in the daily lives of your employees: safety, on-time delivery, and profitability on a small scale, such as daily or weekly. If the small goals are met, the big goals will fall in place, too.

Question – How will employees know how they're doing with regard to materials versus budget?

Answer – Simple: OVER communicate.

How –Hold kick-off meetings, post daily ticker reports, and have job cost meetings, as well as performance reviews, after shipment.

Question – How do we relay expectations?

Answer – OVER communicate.

How –Constructive criticism and praise throughout the project. Consider having monthly employee input meetings, with management updates.

Access the Electronic Resource Hub

Scan the QR code to see more about the employee input meeting

I love the employee input meetings at Wisconsin Oven Corporation!

Finance is all about the scoreboard update and it's critical to have finance as a part of the planning in all areas of the company because so many things are attached. Consider some of these questions: What are we able to afford? What's the current cash flow versus the profit and loss? What capital investments can we make that will give us a great return on investment?

At Wisconsin Oven, particularly with regard to the financial processes, we needed to implement a measuring system. Without a play clock or scores, it's hard for a team to really see how well they're doing, or how much more work needs to be done to achieve a goal (and by what time).

Our scoreboards were put up in the different departments and they measured our orders, our deadlines, our budget, and other important data. It was a way for the team to, at a glance, know how close they were to achieving victory on a number of metrics.

From the time of its implementation, the scoreboard was talked about in meetings. Meetings are one of those necessary rituals of business, regardless of culture. Early in the company, there was a lot of attendance, but no passion. Under our second regime, a typical employee meeting was held after hours, had four to six people in attendance and had no input from the teams who would be implementing the decisions being made.

Our culture had changed. It was time that our meetings did, too! I wanted to get the same overwhelming team energy that I thought was becoming present in the rest of our daily operations.

Our initial goal with the process questions we asked ourselves was to help us to create strategies WE needed to improve existing processes and develop new ones that could result in:

"Passion"

Passion combines effort, positivity, and your will for a purpose.

~Dave's Definitions

- Finding New Markets
- Increasing Sales
- Implementing Lean Manufacturing
- Creating Departmental Goals
- Setting Individual Goals
- Developing A Means To Measure And Evaluate The Company And Team Members

Like just about every other subject on the planet, there is a "Dummies" book for coaching. More specifically, there are articles about how to motivate football players.

> *"Football is the ultimate team game, and you need to motivate your players to work as a team. Although the sport allows individuals in some positions (such as quarterbacks, who can elude defenders and scramble downfield) to create plays on their own, you and your team are much better off if you can get everyone to work together as a cohesive unit on the field.*
>
> *Finding a surefire route to teaching the essence of teamwork among your players is difficult. Try getting the players to begin seeing the enormous benefits that accompany working as a team (rather than as a bunch of individuals) . . . "*

The article isn't about professional ball, so it obviously doesn't go on to talk about financial rewards. It addresses instead that what fuels us are things such as praise and brotherhood. The real surprise is that what fuels us as kids really isn't any different than what fuels us as adults.

Getting the right people in the right positions and the right leaders managing those people answers the who of professional growth. Getting the processes in place answers the what of professional growth. Simon Sinek, in his book "Start With Why" gets to the heart of the matter by asking us to imagine a world where people wake up inspired to go to work. Without the "why," professional development is as to score you a touchdown as taking a knee. What drives us to move the chains is what I needed to find.

One day, it just became obvious to me that all of us have something that fuels our engine. Money is absolutely on that list and it's naïve to pretend otherwise. But money is not the only thing on the list. I sat down and began to think about all of the things that motivated me and my teams over the years and what I came up with was a "top ten" playbook that I needed to follow if I ever wanted my team to follow the playbook I was creating for them:

1) Delivering Happiness To Internal And External Customers
2) A Simple "Thank You" Or Pat On The Back From A Manager Or High-Level Leader
3) Recognition In Front Of Your Peers
4) Company Published Recognition Noticing Work Accomplished Or Improved
5) Celebration Together As A Team
6) Seeing How Quality Products And Services Lead To New Opportunities
7) The Feeling Of Momentum And Forward Progress
8) Job Security As A Direct Result Of Efforts Expended
9) Support For Non-Work-Related Endeavors From Colleagues
10) Money

Recognizing my own playbook meant that I put into place a new policy of celebrating *everything*. Celebration truly is at the center of a Championship Culture. And, in addition to creating celebrations, I actually went to the leaders and teams to get their input on what sort of reward systems they wanted in place. Our old meetings were called "Employee Input Meetings" and that resulted in people not wanting to speak in front of a large group. The new "all employee meeting" offers the same input, but also provided opportunity for the company to give updates, provide a vision, and lead . . . CELEBRATION!

- There were bonuses put in place and those bonus-earning employees would get recognized in front of their employees by our leadership team!
- We would feature employee photos on the website and in our lobby with written recognition of their accomplishments.
- Simple things such as work anniversaries, new employees, promotions, and retirements were marked with pomp and circumstance.
- We began using a traveling trophy for outstanding employees.
- Team wins would equal a lunch on the company followed by a PAID afternoon off.
- Intra-company contests and healthy competitions and rivalries were encouraged.
- When vendors treated us with gifts such as sporting events or other activities, we would pass those along to employees.
- We worked together on philanthropic causes about which we could feel proud.
- We began holding company events . . . a LOT of company events . . . for every reason we could think of: annual picnics, Christmas parties, lunches for smaller holidays such as Veteran's Day.

- My management team came to me with the idea of our "Spin The Wheel" that we allow high-performing team members to spin at our all employee meetings. On it, there is everything from half and full days off paid, to $25 to $100 gift cards, to event tickets.

left: 5 wooden nickels earns an employee a chance to "Spin the Wheel"
right: the W.O.C Wheel

Our "Spin The Wheel" tradition was an idea that came from direct team leaders and it became one of the most exciting parts of our meetings. Not only do team members want to be at our meetings, now they are watching the scoreboard in anticipation of being recognized in the meetings. ***They have a desire to be champions!***

If there's a bad scoreboard, we go back to the processes. We adjust. We improve with each new challenge. We work the play until we score . . . as a team.

top: Veteran's Day lunch;
bottom: Christmas party

****

The minute I started implementing this new system of celebration—my championship culture—there was a pushback. It's an investment to kick off a reward system for the first time that is a risk no matter how much you hope and believe it will work. AND . . . the recession had begun.

I've seen over the years that companies invest a ton of money in seminars and employee training. I've seen those who drop a ton of money in consultants. Those development tools in general are good, but they're around for a week. With a consultant, you might get two weeks. Companies can sometimes learn great things despite these resources being from outside of their industries. For most lessons to become a habit, though, you need to practice for three weeks or more.

I find a majority of those types of professional development investments to be a waste of money.

Wouldn't it be better to work in a situation where it's positive every day; not a single day or even a week or two, but your team is positive 365-days a year? Shouldn't your team experience something every single day, even if it's a smile or a handshake? When all of this is positive stuff that gets into your team, it comes out of them. It's a life fuel. It's not a two-day seminar. It's not a fourteen-day training program; it's something that they'll live every day. The whole company can thrive in a championship culture.

Access the Electronic Resource Hub

Scan the QR code for an employee testimonial

****

Favre who? To walk around just about any part of Wisconsin on a fall or winter Sunday, you would never guess the painstaking transition that was required for Green Bay Packer fans to accept Aaron Rodgers to take over as our green and gold leader. You wouldn't know that, in the year Favre returned wearing the rival purple and yellow colors of the Minnesota Vikings, fans in Lambeau were holding up bitter signs that read "12 Is Three Times Better than 4!" The focus then was on beating down the old king in favor of the new.

Brett Favre may have set a Prima Dona precedent, but he helped to build a foundation in which today's very beloved Aaron Rodgers could flourish. The Packers earned their trip to Super Bowl XLV against the Pittsburgh Steelers. Rodgers completed twenty-four of thirty-nine pass attempts for three hundred four yards and three touchdowns! He was named MVP of the Super Bowl and NFL Player of the Year for the 2010 season. Rodgers became only the third player in NFL history to pass for over 1,000 yards in a single postseason (1094 total, to be exact) and also became one of only four quarterbacks to record over three hundred yards passing, with at least three touchdown passes, and no interceptions in a Super Bowl. The Packers pulled out a 31-25 win against the Steelers and, on that day, Aaron Rodgers became the new king of a new era of victory.

****

In the recession, we didn't have the resources we wanted, but people understood and, in a culture where we were family, people worked together to get through it. We supported each other.

We maintained all of the non-fiscal cultural investments we could during the recession.

We communicated every loss together as a team.

We spread the pain and bore the burden of our tight period with more grace than old regime teams often bore victories.

I worked for free or for one third pay.

All of the high paid leadership worked at one third pay.

This sacrificial attitude is a big reason for why I still have that leadership team, today.

We asked team members who wanted to take a voluntary day off, without pay, once a month and that effort was shared among many. The following year was a record year followed by another record year!

*I love our annual tradition of celebrating success. In 2015, we celebrated
with a live radio broadcast on the "Bob and Brian Morning Show"*

Access the Electronic Resource Hub

*Scan the QR code to see a video of the company shouting:
"WE ARE THE CHAMPIONS" on live morning drive time radio;
with the "Bob and Brian Morning Show", 102.9 The HOG FM*

Championship Culture at W.O.C.

I love celebrating our monthly Work of Champions winners!

W.O.C in the Community

top: driving the W.O.C. float in the East Troy, WI summer parade
bottom: helping the East Troy Police Dept. encourage teens' safe driving

W.O.C. Ice Bucket Challenge!

Access the Electronic Resource Hub

*Scan the QR code to see more about
the Ice Bucket Challenge*

DID YOU KNOW?

NFL REFEREES RECEIVE SUPER BOWL RINGS, TOO.

NEVER UNDERESTIMATE THE VALUE OF MAKING THE TOUGH CALLS!

<u>Overtime</u>

I remember the day we took the photo on the cover of the book. It was OUR biggest comeback celebration. The Buffalo Bills had nothing on us. We had a project that really clogged up our shop.

The job we were behind on was for two very large ovens sold to Ford® Motor Company and they took up 65% to 70% of our entire shop floor. To make matters worse, we completely under-quoted the custom build. We sold them for about half of what we should have done. Both of the ovens took way too long. Also, like many other major corporations, the payment terms don't cover the financing of the project. We called these two ovens "the twins" and—from order to shipment—we had them in house for a full year undergoing engineering, safety, and production Not only did we have capacity issues, but we were late, and—because of the bottleneck on our shop floor—we had to subcontract.

The twins tied up **everything**. We were behind on **everything**. We, as a team, had **nothing** left to give.

At the end of one of many unprofitable months during "the twins" residency, I pulled my top ten performers into a meeting with lunch on our then-unprofitable company, gave them all raises, and told them I needed them to champion a strong finish for the two ovens within their teams.

Then, at one of our company meetings, we held a real rally. We played an inspirational video: Al Pacino giving his famous speech from "Any Given Sunday." We were, as the speech famously said, in the midst of the biggest battle of our professional lives. We needed to "fight our way back" one inch at a time. The team had to look for inches to get us through!

We got creative with a flea-flicker maneuver of our own. We had another company with some space, technically a competitor, and we subcontracted to them with some of our people to go over and show them how to build our standard products. They signed non-disclosures, but it was still risky; this was crisis management. How were we going to make customers happy? This trick play was what we needed. We still have a relationship with that industry brother today.

It took three more months to deliver "the twins."

Access the Electronic Resource Hub

Scan the QR code for a customer testimonial

*In Pacino's speech, he talked about living being the six **inches** in front of our faces, but we went through six **months** of misery . . . to get six months of results. The results were more than just making it through the project. Shipping meant that we had our most profitable and most productive time in company history. More than that, though, it was the highest MORALE our team had ever experienced. That day, we celebrated our blitz with a blitz of our own. We had WON big in overtime!*

I loved getting to cut the ribbon on our championship expansion!

Access the Electronic Resource Hub

Scan the QR code to see more about Wisconsin Oven's expansion

Field Goal

"Sports and business go hand-in-hand. Both entail risk of loss and involve hard work to accomplish goals. Competitive athletes and entrepreneurs have a lot in common."

~Nicole Coulter

Kickers are some of the most underrated players on a football team. They don't have all of the drama on their plays. Everybody knows where the ball is going, for the most part. If you're lucky, a kicker can bring in three points. Those three points can mean a win more often than not, though. According to NFL market analyst, Andrew Brocker, a full 75% of NFL games that go into overtime are won by a field goal.

Finding three safe points to move your team forward can be the difference between a championship and a loss. Here are a few three-point recaps from *"Building A Championship Culture."*

3-Points – Find Lessons For Business Through:

1. Competition
2. Observing Effort
3. Taking Risks

3-Points – Work Your Way Toward Leadership Through:

1. Trust
2. Smarter AND Harder Efforts
3. Mentorship

3-Points - Standard Expectations That Lead To Results:

1. Showing Up Every Day
2. Showing Up On Time
3. Having A Pleasant Attitude

Culture is the heartbeat of any and all businesses and teams. It's not the product, the building, or the strategy; it's the people. The people have to have shared vision, strong leadership, and the ability to work as a team. That team has to have developed strength relating to one another just by being together. Leadership and team members must have instilled confidence in one another that they are there for one another.

3-Points – A Championship Culture For Products:

1. Remember Your Target Demographic
2. Remove Distractions
3. Change With The Times

3-Points – A Championship Culture For People:

1. SCOUT Your Team Players For Competencies And Skills
2. PLAYER COACH Your Team Players To Effectively Play Their Positions
3. HEAD COACH The Whole Team Through A Willingness To Change Player Positions

"Team" and "Family"

There's really no difference between team and family. In order for a family to function well, it needs to operate like a team. In order for a team to function well, it needs to operate like a family.

~Dave's Definitions

3-Points – A Championship Culture For Process:

1. Have Administrative Processes That Make The Playbook Known And Game Plan Understood By All Players
2. Use Operational Processes To Streamline Your Departments From Order Inception To Shipment
3. OVER-Communicate Financial Processes Through A Scoreboard

Above all, in the words of Henry Kubicki,

"Build your team. Finish clean."

Champion Your Own Life

Playing On The Home Field

> *"I firmly believe that any man's finest hour, the greatest fulfillment of all that he holds dear, is that moment when he has worked his heart out in a good cause and he lies exhausted on the field of battle - victorious."*
> **~Vince Lombardi**

In 2015, Wisconsin Oven became a brand of Thermal Product Solutions (TPS). The acquisition led to Wisconsin Oven joining four other leading industrial brands and being a part of a group that offers equipment across the full spectrum of thermal needs from -112 degrees F to 3200 degree furnaces. There are solutions for every heating and cooling need under TPS.

I am now the Chief Executive Officer of the full group and the goal now is to be the overall leader in the entire thermal industry. Across all of the TPS brands, I am working on implementing a championship culture.

The generosity of a championship culture has helped me learn that it's not what you get in life, it's what you give and everything else takes care of itself.

With my family, when anybody is in a time of need, I can help. My incredible wife, Andrea, and I live by that philosophy. We do what we're able to for our families and friends.

top to bottom: stepdaughters Chloe, Ava, wife Andrea, and me

In life, just as in business, it's about what you can do with great people. As a leader, it is my hope to always identify the great in people so that I can coach them toward a championship.

It is my enduring honor to be the *Head Coach Of A Championship Culture* and to help you serve in that position for your teams.

Snapshots...

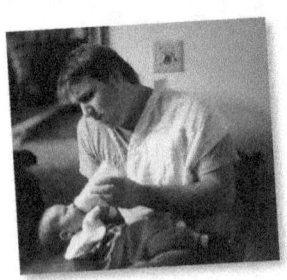

Acknowledgements

It's amazing when I look back on life and see snapshots of experiences that I thought to be so minor at the time, and now realize what major events they were in my life. I have to say that Mr. Henry Kubicki, the founder of Wisconsin Oven Corporation, created something special for many people. I am thankful that I happened to be one of those people who, as a teenager in 1986, stumbled in the door to fill out an application. He's one of the faces frozen as a snapshot in my memory

Next, I imagine a picture of Bruce Champion, the man that hired me; he gambled on this kid with very limited experience and a mullet that might suggest he belong jamming out in a hair band rather than working as a responsible dedicated employee. Bruce was a mentor in the workplace and in life. I have no doubt that, if it were not for Bruce's dedication to build people, I would not be writing this book, today. Bruce taught me and my peers the art of positive thinking, visualization, goal-setting, and creating and executing affirmations. Bruce taught me the value of building a worker's confidence through recognition and sincere interest in the personal lives of those on a team.

In another snapshot in my memory, I remember myself barely able to walk to the time clock. My shirt in those days was usually soaked with sweat and even my breath smelled like paint. My arms had a perpetual rash from the fiberglass-filled insulation I worked with every fourteen-hour day. I was sure to be very useless to my family when I finally reached the doorstep. My children would often be found climbing over me while I was passed out on the couch despite the ever-prevalent rash and stained hands from painting and metalwork.

My kids were my rock; they were my purpose for getting up again at 4:00 A.M. and doing it all over again the next day. As time went on, I would miss many school events, teacher conferences, and quality parenting opportunities. I did the best I could with family time when we had time, but they definitely did the best they could all the time.

In a later snapshot, I'm reminded of a very sad day when I saw my dear friend and boss walking down the road with his tie off and his head hanging low. I knew that it was his last day of employment. The glory of my promotion was tainted by the sadness of my dear friend's departure from Wisconsin Oven. Hank created opportunity for those who dedicated their lives to the cause of the company, but it was his way or the highway.

I turn the page in my mind to the next snapshot and I see a team that rallied behind me. They believed in me and the vision of Wisconsin Oven to become the best in the world. I was truly blessed to be surrounded with such talented, hardworking, dedicated individuals!

A more recent snapshot I picture is the first day I met Emeran Leonard, who is the Chairman of my TEC group (The Executive Committee). Twenty years of experience at everything except the position of President & CEO, found me looking for resources to help me with this new endeavor. TEC is like an extended board of directors. They are all CEOs with a ton of experience. We all share our experience, and our goal is to help all in our group succeed. Great resource speakers, great business experience, and we all hold each other accountable. No question, TEC is the single most powerful resource I ever made the decision to sign up for. I credit the great CEOs in TEC 18 for being the most powerful influence in the last 10 years of my career, and they are all near and dear to my heart! In addition to Emeran, thank you to Andy Burkhart, President and CEO of Burkhart Heisdorf Insurance, Dirk Debbink, Chairman and CEO of MSI General, Tom Engler President of 3e Mobile Solutions, Ann Hanna, Managing Director of Schenk M&A Solutions, Bob Hartline, President and CEO of Xymox Technologies, Inc., Jay Hogfeldt, President of Wind Mill Slatwall Productions, Bruce Laning, Managing Director and Principal of Bronfman E.L. Rothschild, Shane Lauterbach, CEO and President of Lauterbach Group, Deni Naumann, President of Copesan Services, Inc., Dave Nestingen, CEO of IEWC, Chris Olson, President and CEO of T-Lon Products, Inc., Phil Rose, President of Roman Electric Company, Inc., Deb Teglia President of Black Diamond Group, Inc., Todd White, President and CEO of Design House, and Steve Ziegler, Chairman of INPRO Corporation.

Then, there is the woman who is in the trenches with me, side-by-side, every day working toward our championship successes! Andrea, I thank you for your unwavering support over the years. There is nothing easy about living with a man like me and my insane schedule. I thank you for the late evenings helping me finish up all those slideshow presentations. I thank you for the patience in putting up with all of my last minute changes after we think the presentations are done, too!   Thank you for your 17 years of dedication to Wisconsin Oven Corporation's success in your many roles, on and off the clock. Your heart was and continues to be dedicated to the success of Wisconsin Oven Corporation, and now Thermal Product Solutions. Your accomplishments as the head of our marketing for the corporation are to be much credited for the reinvention of our brand at a critical point in the company's history. Thank you for your help and support in writing  this book during a very stressful time in our lives. Finding time for a book with our schedules is only made possible because of our love for one another, and your continued support. Thank you, Andrea, most of all, for being my wife. I love you with all of my heart and soul! You are my number one partner in my career and in my life and my very best friend.

In short, *"Building A Championship Culture,"* the process and the book, would not be possible without my having been surrounded by a championship team in so many areas of my life.

To all of those listed here, and to the many more written on my heart, I offer my sincere gratitude. Thank you for being my champions.

~Dave

Resources

Bach, Greg. *Coaching Football for Dummies*. Indianapolis, IN: Wiley Pub., 2006. Print.

Champion, Bruce. "Profile of a Coach." Personal interview. 31 July 2015.

Collins, James C. *Good to Great: Why Some Companies Make the Leap-- and Others Don't*. New York, NY: Harper Business, 2001. Print.

"Famous Quotes." *BrainyQuote*. Xplore. Web. 9 Oct. 2015.

"Industrial Ovens From The Leader In The Industry." *Industrial Oven Manufacturer*. Web. 9 Oct. 2015.

Kent, Jeff. "Profile of a Captain." Telephone interview. 29 Sept. 2015.

"Official Website of Brett Favre - Packers Hall of Fame Quarterback." *Official Website of Brett Favre - Packers Hall of Fame Quarterback*. Web. 9 Oct. 2015.

Professional Football Hall Of Fame. Web. 9 Oct. 2015.

Sinek, Simon. *Start with Why: How Great Leaders Inspire Everyone to Take Action*. New York: Portfolio, 2009. Print.

Strand, Kurt. "Profile of a Teammate." Telephone interview. 27 Aug. 2015.

About The Authors

Dave Strand, a husband to Andrea and father of three in southeastern Wisconsin, is President and Chief Executive Officer of Thermal Processing Solutions (TPS), LLC. Dave has nearly 30 years of experience in the industrial oven and furnace industry, spanning the areas of operations, service, and sales, all with Wisconsin Oven Corporation, recently acquired by TPS. Dave also serves as President and CEO of Wisconsin Oven, a subsidiary of TPS.

In addition to his considerable experience in the industrial oven and furnace industry, Dave has demonstrated great strategic skill and leadership in driving growth. As President and CEO, Dave led the evolution and growth of Wisconsin Oven from a small standard oven 3rd party manufacturer, to a highly respected designer and manufacturer of custom and standard industrial ovens, in addition to achieving record sales regularly. Dave grew the Wisconsin Oven brand during his tenure despite all of the challenges of the Great Recession. Dave is a respected and often-sought speaker on the subject of company culture.

(Dave is a Packers fan. Reji....is not.)

Working with Dave to create his book was author, Reji Laberje, of Reji Laberje Author Programs, LLC, where their vision is to use meaningful writing to, for, and from you to make far-reaching, positive impacts.
*Learn more at **www.rejilaberje.com**.*

www.ingramcontent.com/pod-product-compliance
Lightning Source LLC
Chambersburg PA
CBHW051916170526
45168CB00001B/407